MIND
HACKING
SECRETS

*Control Thinking, Improve Decision
Making, Reclaim Your Attention,
and Unlock Your Limitless Potential*

SOM BATHLA

www.sombathla.com

Your Free Gift

As a token of my thanks for taking out time to read my book, I would like to offer you a free gift:

Click Below and Download your **Free Report**

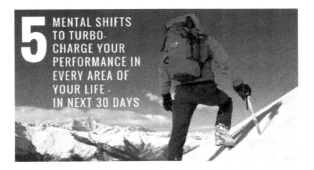

Learn 5 Mental Shifts To Turbo-Charge Your Performance In Every Area Of Your Life - in Next 30 Days!

You can also grab your FREE GIFT Report through this below URL:

http://sombathla.com/mentalshifts

More Books by Som Bathla

Discover Your Why

The Gift of Grit

The Magic Of Accelerated Learning

The Power of Self Discipline

The Science of High Performance

The Way To Lasting Success

The Mindful Mind

Conquer Your Fear Of Failure

The Mindset Makeover

Living Beyond Self Doubt

Focus Mastery

Just Get It Done

Master Your Day Design Your Life

The Quoted Life

The 30- Hour Day

You may also visit my all books together at

http://sombathla.com/amazon

Table of Contents

Introduction

Have you ever thought about questions like these?

- Can I have a perfect memory?
- Is it possible to delete past memories and reprogram my mind with new ones at will?
- Can I tenfold my pace of learning and gain more knowledge and wisdom in less time?
- Is there a way to have brain-to-brain communication, so I know how to understand others' perspectives and have a win-win proposition in any situation?
- Would it be possible to experience what it is like to be someone in the 1800s by purchasing that experience from someone else and installing in your brain?

No doubt, most of us have thought about a few of the questions listed above, but probably not about all of them.

However, there are people who are seriously researching into hacking the brain's power in a massive way by using high-end technology, so they could reprogram it to the maximum benefit of mankind.

Mind Hacking with Technology

An example of one such person is Bryan Johnson, an American entrepreneur in his 40s, who founded a neurotechnology company named Kernel—with a belief that in the next 15 years, humans will be able to greatly expand their brain's natural abilities. As reported[1], Johnson stated that the questions posed above would not appear to be surprising in the next two decades, because he expects the researchers to develop such brain tools, which will significantly enhance the human brain's abilities.

Let's understand how he plans to do it. His company, Kernel, intends to develop a tiny implantable chip in the human brain called "neuroprosthetic" primarily to help people suffering from damages caused by strokes

---

[1] https://bigthink.com/paul-ratner/this-startup-plans-to-put-chips-into-human-brains-to-enhance-intelligence

and Alzheimer's disease. However, from the future perspective, they plan to develop such chips for brain's "cognitive enhancement" through the reprogramming of the human mind to perform significantly better.

Seems pretty intriguing, doesn't it?

And it's not only Johnson, there are other people who are on a similar mission to hack the human mind's potential. Elon Musk, founder of the space research organization SpaceX and the founder of Tesla, also reported[2] about his plans to merge human brains with computers. His team is working on a technology called "Neural Lace" as a way for humans to interact with machines. They plan to implant electrodes in human brains that will send and receive thoughts back and forth to computers like uploading and downloading files. The primary benefit of this technology will be to ameliorate the cognitive functions of human brain, including memory. This neural lace will be like an extra layer on our usual human intelligence.

[2] https://bigthink.com/paul-ratner/elon-musk-creates-new-company-to-merge-human-brains-with-computers

Also, social media giant, Facebook's Mark Zuckerberg doesn't want to lose any opportunity to get the maximum out of human brain. Reports state Facebook is working on a non-invasive "brain-computer speech-to-text interface" that uses "optical imaging" to read the signals of neurons as they form words, find a way to translate those signals into code, and then send the code to a computer. And if this works, it's going to be possible to "type" 100 words a minute just by thinking.

All of that sounds pretty interesting, doesn't it?

Who doesn't want to have a brain that operates like a super computer? We all would love to just implant a chip in our brains and gain all knowledge and experience that otherwise will take years. People are ready to get in a queue tomorrow morning to buy such technology if available, just like they do in front of Apple stores to buy the latest release of any Apple gadget.

But here is the thing. Though neuroscience has already made massive progress in understanding the brain parts and their respective functions with the advent of technology like function magnetic resource imaging (fMRI) and many others (and the research is still on), controlling fully the mind's unique abilities like imagination, creativity, and memory is still a long way off. Also, it's arguable whether the human mind, which generated the technology, can be controlled completely by the advancements of technology—meaning there is no assurance to what extent researchers can extract from this most complex organ in the universe: our mind.

There is a Self-Reliant and Better Way

You'd ask what else you could do to harness the vast potential of your mind. Can you hack your mind on your own without relying too heavily on technology?

Let's explore this. We all know the human brain is the most complex organ in our body, weighing just 2% of our body weight but consumes more than 20% of energy. It is only this human brain that has created all this massive technology to make our lives comfortable. You see all the inventions around you: your mobile phone, satellite television, airplanes, spaceships, internet, advanced equipment for treating ailments, etc. How did all this happen? Of course, all of this is the manifestation of our mind's unexplainably huge potential. It means "whatever the man of mind can conceive and believe, it can achieve," as Napoleon Hill rightly said.

Therefore, the human mind capable of inventing and implementing the most complex technological advancements is itself capable enough to provide the solutions to all your human quests— including the desire to reprogram and expand its potential for human benefits.

This is definitely a better idea. You don't need to wait for any technological innovation. Let the neuroscientists and researchers continue their research, and we will gear up to look inside and understand our own minds, its way of operation, and then upgrade it to unlock the hidden huge potential.

The very objective of this book is to help you understand your own mind's operations and the strategies and techniques used by super-achievers already to hack your own mind. Once you read this book and understand the principles and strategies stated, you will nod your head (as I did researching this topic) to the below quote:

> *"You don't have to be a genius to find the hidden potential deep in your mind." — Ray Davies*

Finally, I'll be candid here to set your expectations right in the beginning. Don't expect this book to be a technical or scientific book about the human brain (remember, we just agreed to let the neuroscientists and brain researchers do this work). Treat this book as something written by just a regular guy who loves to research and explore the mind, human psychology, and behaviour to figure out the ways to optimize his life and is on the journey to help others learn the same. However, having said that, you'll definitely find interesting scientific research and the personal life examples of people we all admire to substantiate arguments in support of the techniques and strategies suggested in the book.

OK, now let's get straight into the subject.

Chapter 1: You Are Not Your Mind

****

"Whatever the mind of man can conceive and believe, it can achieve."

~ Napoleon Hill

Three Layers of the Human Body

Let's start with the basics. The outermost layer of our body is the body parts we can see—our head, face, arms, legs, etc. The next layer of our body is the inside organs of our body, which we can't see (and frankly we don't want to see): your brain, heart, liver, intestines, blood, etc.; they perform specific functions to keep our body alive and moving around. I know, all of this is not some enlightening piece of information, but just hang on for the sake of understanding some further point I want to elaborate.

The above are just two layers with physical visibility. The outer body parts can be seen immediately, while the inner body organs can be seen upon incision of the body, if necessary.

Now coming specifically to the human brain as part of the second layer, neuroscience has already found that the human brain has around 100 billion neurons. And we have hundreds of trillions of neuro-connections between these neurons inside our brain. You wouldn't even want to try to count the number of zeroes here. If we imagine all the stars in the Milky Way, there are more connections in our brain than all of those stars combined. And what is more amazing is that no two brains are exactly alike. That's the level of complexity of our physical brains.

If the physical body parts outside is the first layer, and the internal organs including our brain is the second layer of human body, then the third layer is the human mind— intangible stuff we can't see, but this stays with us all the time.

It's invisible, but a powerful driving force that is behind all human actions, all progress and development. For a book about hacking the mind, it is necessary to understand the boundaries and interplay of roles between our brain and our mind, so let's quickly examine this. Our brain and mind can be compared to a computer.

A computer requires hardware (screen monitor, CPU (Central Processing Unit) box, keyboard, mouse, etc.) to at least operate the machine part. But this hardware needs software (Windows or Mac operating software (OS)) to make it run. Without software, hardware would be useless, and without hardware, the software would be useless. Your brain is like the hardware and your mind is like its software.

With the hardware of the brain, you coordinate your moves, your various physiological processes, your day-to-day activities, and transmit impulses. Every living creature has a brain that is necessary to perform such functions that are necessary to survive. All animals feel hunger, thirst, and other necessary body functions, and their brain triggers the necessary behavior for that. But, as a human, you use the mind to think. The mind is the manifestation of thoughts, perceptions, emotions, determinations, memories, and imagination—and all of this takes place within the brain. The mind is the awareness of consciousness we know, the ability to control what we do, and to know what we are doing and why; it's the ability to understand. Lower animals are able only to *interpret* their environments on a basic level, but they *do not understand* them, whereas humans can understand what happens around them, even if they don't find any scientific reasoning for it. It's only the mind which has made humans capable of solving complex problems, which differentiates them from the other living creatures. Our ability to analyze situations makes it possible to develop solutions to problems and lead us toward practical solutions.

You see, we are moving from simplest to complex levels, from tangible to intangible. The outside physical body, the internal body organs, and our mind—these are the three layers of our human body or existence. But there is some further layer too. Let's talk about that.

The Fourth Layer

Your mind is not the last layer of your existence. There's something more that is also not only physically invisible, but you can't even comprehend or think about its existence like your mind.

What's that? Let's try this with an example.

Assuming your hand gets hurt, how do you describe it? No brainer, you say, "your hand" got hurt. When you have a stomach trouble, you say "your stomach" is aching.

Similarly, when you are not able to think properly or you're mentally fatigued, what do you say? You say "your mind" is tired or not working optimally.

You see, in all these three levels of our body, tangible or intangible, there is one commonality. You used a common word to show that something belong to you or you have control upon: "your" hand, "your" stomach, or "your" mind. You didn't differentiate your "intangible mind" from your other "tangible organs." You considered all three levels as something that you own or control.

Therefore, the logical conclusion is: There is a level beyond these three levels that owns these three layers of your existence. Now, don't be surprised when I say you're reading this book about hacking "your" mind only—it means there is someone or something else who will hack your mind.

Who is there at level four?

That's your consciousness. OK, just hang on, a bit of clarification before you start thinking something else. No, I'm not getting into spirituality, religion, faith, or anything mystical. I'm just trying to peel off the layers of your existence, so that we can look at the root and start from the foundation. At the deepest layer is your consciousness, the supreme power or infinite intelligence or whatever you may want to call it, and all three layers of your existence belong to the fourth level of our existence.

You need to deeply understand that you are not your mind; there's something else that can observe the mind. This something is "you"," the consciousness, which is separate from your mind. The fact that you can observe your mind and think about it objectively shows there is a "mind," and then an "observer of the mind."

Your Mind is like a Movie Playing in Your Head

Let's understand "you" and "your mind" as separate with the help of one example. Understanding this difference is so fundamental for hacking your mind, but it is entirely missing in our everyday lives. Sir John Hargrave, an entrepreneur, comedian, and author of the book *Mind Hacking: How to Change Your Life in 21 Days,* compares your mind with a movie. Assume you are watching a movie—a very engaging one—and you are completely immersed in the movie. It might happen that for few moments you will feel as if you are part of the movie. Maybe you'll find yourself crying watching some sad scene in the movie or maybe you get spooked by watching some gory scenes there. But in reality, it's you who is watching the movie being displayed only on the screen.

With the same analogy, your mind is also a movie that's being played in your head, and you are watching the thoughts running in your mind. Just like you are completely lost in a wonderfully created piece of cinema and your thoughts, emotions, and sensations were all in constant stream with the movie, the same happens with your "mind movie." And it's not an ordinary movie, its way more than your outside 3D Dolby digital sound with all high-tech or sci-fi effects. And on top of it, it's being played in your head non-stop since your birth.

Therefore, you are so accustomed to watching it and the worst part is—no one ever told you that it's just a movie being played in your own head. The movie is created by a continuous infiltration of emotions, feelings, and thoughts of people around us, in every waking hour of our life—and that's why it is no wonder the movie has engrossed us so well.

In your journey toward hacking your mind, this distinction that you are separate from your mind is very important, because only then would you be able to experiment on your mind as a subject of exploration.

I hope the distinction between the four levels of your existence and the analogies above helped you to disengage with your mind and see it from a distance. It's the first prerequisite of controlling your mind that you should be able to see it objectively.

Before we get into understanding the operating system of our mind, another important aspect is understanding the huge potential of invisible power called the mind.

Understand Your Mind's Massive Potential

The mind is a hidden superpower that has enabled man to travel to space and land on the moon. The days are not far when human beings will be residing on planet Mars.

But it's not true that only a few humans have such immense mind power. Rather, it is available to every one of us. Unfortunately, a few decades ago, the common understanding was that human intelligence is limited; people believed that the human mind has fixed capacity from birth, and it can't be changed any further. But thanks to the research conducted in the field of neuroscience and human psychology, we have come to know the concept of neuroplasticity. The good news is that science has concluded there is no such thing such as a fixed or only-once wired mind. Rather, it has the potential to keep changing during one's lifetime, thanks to the awareness about the concept of neuroplasticity.

Neuroplasticity is the ability of your brain to reorganize itself, both physically and functionally, throughout your life due to changes in your environment, behavior, thinking, and emotions. With the recent capability to visually "see" into the brain with the help of the fMRI, science has confirmed the incredible morphing ability of the brain beyond any doubt.

Dr. Michael Merzenich, author of *Soft-Wired: How the New Science of Brain Plasticity Can Change Your Life*, has stated with proven research that no one is stuck merely with the brain which they are born with. Norman Doidge further explains the concept of our brain's elasticity in his book *The Brain That Changes Itself: Stories of Personal Triumph from the Frontiers of Brain Science* below:

> "The brain Dr. Merzenich describes is not an inanimate vessel that we fill; rather it is more like a living creature with an appetite, one that can grow and change itself with proper nourishment and exercise.

> Before Merzenich's work, the brain was seen as a complex machine, having unalterable limits on memory processing speed, and intelligence. Merzenich has shown that each of these assumptions is wrong."

I recently came across one miraculous life story of a little girl named Cameron Mott[3], from North Carolina, which proves the vast potential of neuroplasticity on our body's abilities.

Just after her third birthday, Cameron started having violent seizures. They became worse and worse, and eventually she was losing her ability to speak. Doctors diagnosed her with something called Rasmussen's encephalitis, a rare inflammatory neurological disease, and the only real treatment for this was hemispherectomy—cutting out half of her brain.

The impact of this surgery was to be very catastrophic for this girl. Because one half of your brain controls and is responsible for

---

[3] https://www.theconfidentteacher.com/2017/09/a-new-school-year-and-a-new-start/

movement and sensation in the other half of your body, i.e., the left hemisphere controls the right side of your entire body's function, and vice versa. This surgery would immediately leave Cameron hemiplegic, meaning suffering from paralysis of one side of the body due to removing half the brain.

But to the utmost surprise, just four weeks post-operation, she walked out of the hospital. And after few months of difficult rehabilitation, she returned to good health and was again going to school, participating in the school activities, and living a life of miraculous normality. She was free from her seizures after the surgery, and despite having half of her brain removed, she was able to live a normal life.

How could 50% of the brain work almost like 100% for Cameron?

It happened because the remaining part of Cameron's brain sensed the massive loss of neural tissue and it physically rewired and reorganized itself to take over everything that the other half had previously handled.

This proves the vast ability of the brain to change itself—to rewire.

Science has shown that neuroplastic changes happen our entire lives, regardless of age or any other factor. Radical improvements in cognitive function—how we learn, think, perceive, and remember—are possible even in the elderly. **Your brain makes physical changes based on the repetitive things you do and experiences you have**. Now we can say the quote by Jim Rohn has some scientific backing too, when he said, "You are the average of the five people you spend most time with."

Remember, the above two concepts that (1) you are separate from your mind, thus you can control it; and (2) the neuroplasiticity of your brain, which can help you grow as much as you want, are the most important brain tattoos that you need to engrain in your mind. Yes, they are that important, because this understanding and belief about your mind's capabilities will go a long way in your journey to unlock your mind's limitless potential.

With that, let's continue to the next section,

where you'll understand how our minds operate.

Chapter 2: Understand Mind's Operating System

****

"Look past the exterior, and see that there is so much more within. Then decide to unleash that potential to the fullest."

~Lincoln Patz

You already know by now about the complexity of the physical brain. Looking at the sheer number of billions of neurons and trillions of neuro-connections happening among these neurons, you would agree that comparing it with a even with highly complex puzzle created by a super-computer would be a huge understatement.

But thankfully, there has been decent amount of research already conducted in the field of neuroscience that can help us now at least see within the brain about how this complex system works.

A Peek Inside Your Brain

Neuroscientists have peeked inside the human brain to understand what's going on there with the help of many advanced techniques, including the fMRI. They have gone much deeper into the layers of the neuron to see how the process works. The neuron level structure shows that each neuron has a cell body with two components: (1) a single long branch known as the **axon** and (2) multiple shorter branches known as **dendrites**.

One important transaction that happens within the brain is when neurons pass on signals to the other neurons. They do it through touching other neurons, and that junction is called the **synapse**.

Current brain research supports the idea that most learning and development happens in the brain through the strengthening and weakening of these **synaptic connections**. There is some estimation that each neuron may have anywhere from one to ten thousand synaptic connections, and therefore the number of different patterns of possible connections in the brain is about *forty* *quadrillion*, a number that is beyond comprehension of most human beings.

These neurons are the basic functional cells that appear to control learning. They encode, store, and retrieve information as well as influence all aspects of human behavior. Neurons act like tiny batteries sending chemical and electrical signals that create processes to integrate and generate information. The threshold for firing at the synapse is determined by the amount of chemicals (called neurotransmitters) released onto the receiving neurons (Bloom, Nelson, and Lazerson, 2001). At the synapse, these chemicals excite the receiving neurons and cause them to fire, inhibit them from firing, or modify their excitability. Examples of common neurotransmitters are dopamine and epinephrine, which are involved in affecting our emotions and mood.

Whenever we learn something new, that information is stored in the brain through the connections between different neurons. It is only through practice and repetition that we strengthen the connection between the neurons. In fact, neuroscientists have a saying: Neurons that fire together wire together. Apparently, all our learning and information occurs through the connection between the neurons. For example, imagine that a neuron that encodes a place and another that encodes an emotion are activated when a wrong experience is felt at a particular place. As a result of this experience, these two neurons fire together and then wire together. Then, whenever the neurons of this particular place are activated, the emotion is also retrieved. Small networks are connected with other small and large networks to resemble a forest of neuronal networks with tens of thousands of synaptic connections.

All our beliefs and perceptions about circumstances and events in our life is nothing but these synaptic connections between our neurons. Since repetition is the key to developing any particular type of synaptic connection, it gives us power to choose what kinds of neuron connections we want to promote or reduce.

The above explanation shows the neuroscience perspective on how our minds operate at the neuronal level and produce different kind of thoughts, beliefs, and perceptions. Now let's examine the complex operating system of our mind through a human psychology perspective and see how we make decisions.

The Two Systems of Our Mind

We tend to think that we make all decisions rationally, supported by clear logic. But this is far from truth. Not all our decisions are supported by logic and rationale. There are other factors that play a vital role in the decision-making process.

How do you know whether the decisions we make are rational decisions or are simply influenced by our emotions?

Let's try to understand how this operating system works.

Daniel Kahneman, renowned psychologist and Nobel Laureate in Economics, in his book *Thinking, Fast and Slow* explains that we have two different systems operating in our mind that control our decision-making. You can compare this to a drama going on between two characters in your head. These two characters of your mind are (1) the impulsive, automatic, and intuitive **System**

1; and (2) the thoughtful, deliberate, and calculative **System 2**.

As the name indicates, System 1 operates intuitively and suddenly that doesn't demand any conscious control of the mind. For example, if you hear a loud noise around you, you will suddenly jump and immediately your whole attention will shift toward the place from where the noise came. System 1 is part of our brain's evolution process; it was necessary in the primitive age for our survival. Any sound or sudden reaction in our environment could have meant a matter of life or death. Any slight sound of leaves or trees could mean some wild hungry animal assaulting upon us in search of his food. Though that sound might have turned out to be the wind, it was too risky to take that so easily, so System 1 helped us survive in those situations.

On the other hand, System 2 is responsible for executive decision-making, thinking rationally and logically on some subject. System 2 deals with all the conscious activities of our mind, which involves paying attention, controlling your instincts, and focusing on the important work at hand— meaning all activities that require deliberate focus of our mind.

Let's understand the relationship between these two systems of our mind by the famous example of the bat-and-ball problem. Here is the question:

A bat and a ball cost $1.10. The bat costs one dollar more than the ball. Can you answer how much the ball costs?

The immediate response that comes to your mind is: the ball costs $0.10.

Most people in this experiment will choose the above, but this is wrong answer. Now think about it again and try to solve it.

The right answer is that the ball costs $0.05 only. Here what happened was that impulsive System 1 took over and it acted too fast to answer.

Generally, the interplay between System 1 and System 2 works in way that only if System 1 is unable to answer a particular problem, it transfers the same to System 2 for resolution. However, in the bat-and-ball problem, System 1 got tricked. There was an error in judgement, and System 1 assumed that the problem was too simple to be transferred to System 2.

Why did this happen? It's because of the principle known as **the law of least effort**, which reveals our innate mental laziness. In fact, our mind tends to use the minimum amount of energy possible for each task. Because referring the question to System 2 and efforts by System 2 requires energy consumption, System 1 avoided that step to protect the mind's energy.

What should be the right approach?

It's really not the optimum use of our mind to behave mostly in the influence of System 1; rather, it's unfortunate to be guided by this mental laziness. There are studies that show that practicing System 2 tasks like focus and self-control leads to higher intelligence scores. By being lazy and avoiding System 2 intelligence, our mind is limiting the strength of our intelligence.

Just this understanding and awareness that there are two systems in the mind affecting our decision-making process will help you to become a bit more vigilant. Now you will be able to differentiate whether it was

System 1 or System 2 that worked in any particular situation.

Now let's look at another perspective that governs our mind in making any decision.

Experiencing Self vs. Remembering Self

We tend to think about ourselves as a unitary entity, meaning we have a particular perception about ourselves and the things around us, and we strongly believe this as the only right perception. But there is a basic flaw in the way we form and strengthen our own self.

In fact, our minds don't remember the experiences in a straightforward way, rather we have two memory selves; they are called the experiencing self and the remembering self.

The experiencing self is the past records about how we feel about the experience in the present moment. It asks the question, **"How does it feel?"** On the other hand, the remembering self does the job of recording the entire event after the fact. It asks the question, **"How was it on the whole?"**

The experiencing self is the "you" in the moment that lives through the event. The remembering self is the "you" that writes the history. **But it is the remembering self that is consulted when planning the future, not the experiencing self**. Hence, the decisions are made based on the remembering self's construction of what happened in the past.

But the important point to be remembered here is: it is the experiencing self that gives the more accurate account of what happened, because our feelings during an experience are always the most accurate. The remembering self is less accurate, because it registers the memories after the situation is finished. But the problem is that the experiencing self and the remembering self don't agree on what happened, and unfortunately, it is the remembering self that dominates our memory.

In one study[4], the subjects had a hand immersed in ice water at a temperature that

[4]http://journals.sagepub.com/doi/10.1111/j.1467-9280.1993.tb00589.x

caused moderate pain. They were told that they would have three trials. While the hand was in the water, the other hand used a keyboard to continuously record their level of pain. The first trial lasted 60 seconds. The second trial lasted 90 seconds, however in the last 30 seconds the water was slowly warmed by 1 degree (better, but still painful). For the third trial, they were allowed to choose which of the first two trials was less disagreeable, and repeat that one.

Here's what they found. 80% of the subjects who reported experiencing some decrease in their pain in the last 30 seconds of the second trial chose to repeat the 90-second experience! In other words, their remembering self elected the second option that required an additional 30 seconds of suffering.

Here is the conclusion comes out of this experiment and many other experiments conducted in this regard. **Duration of the experiment does not count. It's only the peak (best or worst moment) and the end of the experience that gets registered in our memory, which**

forms the basis for taking our all future decisions.

You must have realized the way our minds operate is not a straightforward calculation like 2+2=4. You don't often make choices based on your rationale or logic, rather emotions play a vital role in affecting your decisions. Let's just briefly touch upon how emotions affect our brain.

Our emotions are processed by the amygdala, a small, almond-shaped brain structure. It responds powerfully to negative emotions, which are regarded as signals of threat. Functional brain imaging has shown that activation of the amygdala by negative emotions interferes with the brain's ability to solve problems or do other cognitive work. Positive emotions and thoughts do the opposite—they improve the brain's executive function and so help open the door to creative and strategic thinking. Therefore, it's a no-brainer that you should choose more positive emotions. You need to try to improve the balance of positive and negative emotions over the course of a day. Barbara Fredrickson, a psychology researcher and author of the book

Positivity recommends a ratio of 3:1 positive to negative emotions. She states that 80% of Americans fall short of the 3:1 positivity ratio that predicts flourishing. You can calculate your own positivity ratio by visiting her website tool at www.positivityratio.com.

OK, so far you have gotten to know what your mind is and how the operating system of your mind works. Now is the time to understand what exactly hacking your mind looks like and for that let's move to the next section.

Chapter 3: What the Heck is Mind Hacking?

"Your mind is your greatest Power. Use it well."

~Aneta Cruz

What Exactly Do We Mean by Mind Hacking?

The dictionary shows two different meanings for the term *hack*. The first definition explains that hacking means to write computer programs for enjoyment. Another definition puts it differently: "to gain access to a computer illegally." But we are not going to do something illegal here by privately stealing the information from someone else's mind. This book is not about hypnotizing somebody else and getting the results you want from that person (though who wouldn't want to control the thinking of their boss and get a hefty salary hike?).

We are accessing and trying to control that data in our own mind—nothing illegal here.

Also, another thing to notice is that the term *hack* has recently entered the general usage with a new non-technological sense, meaning "solution" or "work around" as in the usage "life hack."

But here is the best definition of hacking for the purposes of this book:

Hacker's Dictionary[5] defines the term hacker as "a person who enjoys learning the details of programming systems and how to stretch their capabilities, as opposed to most users who prefer to learn only the minimum necessary."

This book intends to follow the approach suggested in the above definition, which means we will analyze the "source code" of the mind, imagining (based on what we see elsewhere) how best we can make this code to do something different, then reprogramming the code by stretching our own capabilities in order to change our lives for the better.

---

[5] http://www.dourish.com/goodies/jargon.html

You are reading this book because you want to learn the secrets of the complex programming of your mind with the objective to use the maximum potential of your brain for attaining success in your life. You are not here to just understand the bare minimum concept of the mind necessary to operate at a reasonable level because chances are that you are already using your mind's bare minimum capacity for working. You are here to learn the deeper secrets of your mind, and that requires claiming and exercising special rights to get inside your mind, as you will learn now.

Claim the "Admin Rights" to Your Mind

Assume you work in an office environment or any other community-like structure, where many people work together using computers connected through a common server. You might have experienced, while installing some program or software on your computer, seeing a message on your screen stating that you don't have the administration rights to change the computer's pre-existing setting by some new software. Your computer requires you to take permission from the controller of computer's network before you install any third-party software on the computer. You are not granted the rights to change the software settings of the computer because it might adversely affect the whole network, if you inadvertently install some malicious software.

In this case, you have got only the "user" rights, which means you can use the computer only for the limited purposes of doing your work, as determined by the organization or community you work with. But the controller of the network has "admin rights," meaning he or she can make any changes, install or remove any programs or software, or do anything at the computer network level. Therefore, unless you get the admin rights, you can't make any changes in your system.

Similarly, to hack your mind, you need to empower yourself with the *admin* rights; after all, you are going to reprogram your software, install new applications, remove the bugs out of your mind, and anything and everything significant to get the best out of the computer of your mind.

When you keep on working the way you have always worked, based on what your family, school, work environment, or society has taught you to be, you have given yourself the "user" rights of your brain. You are using only the pre-installed system and software, and therefore you are able to do only the limited amount of work and innocently assume that you are delivering your best. It's only when you dare to think beyond what is programmed in your head for ages, that you decide to take charge of your mind and eventually your own world. It's only when you are convinced about the malleability of your brain, about the plastic nature of your mind that you think of transforming yourself into a different and changed human being.

But remember, you have to be all in; lukewarm will not do. If you are super curious to know the complex layers of your brain, if you are prepared to do the experiments with your own mind, if you are ready to put in what it takes to harness the power of your mind, then welcome, you have already got a hold of the admin rights for your mind's software. And no, you don't need to seek permission from someone else.

OK, since you have already assumed the admin rights available to you, let's start the process of hacking your mind to do everything that is needed: uninstalling the old programming, installing the new software, and coding new programs using our imagination to get the best out of us.

Before you can bring in new material, you need to get rid of the obsolete and non-usable items to make space for the novel things. Your old thinking and conditions have bugged your mind, so the first step is to debug your mind, which we will do in the next section of this book.

Chapter 4: How To Debug Your Mind?

****

> *"A man cannot directly choose his circumstances, but he can choose his thoughts, and so indirectly, yet surely, shape his circumstances."*
>
> *~James Allen*

Earlier in the book, you noticed your emotions and other factors play a vital role in your thinking and making important decisions. In this section, we will talk about certain types of thinking patterns that keep you stuck and not let you think in a different and better way.

Your thinking patterns can be compared to loops in the software. In computer programming, a loop is a sequence of instructions that is continually repeated until a certain condition is reached.

These loops of thinking pattern develop through never-ending programming of our beliefs through our surrounding environment. Let's examine this from childhood to adulthood. When you were born, there was nothing on your mind; you were a clean slate. But as you grew up, you looked at the surrounding environment and started to pick up things from them. Your parents started to teach you how to stand, walk, and then run; your teachers taught you how to read numbers and the alphabet; and you and your friends together learned to play and have fun in life.

This all sounds good and of course important. But the problem emerges when you start believing the facts, circumstances, etc. in a particular way, mainly because your parents, friends, or teachers think in that particular way. Society started embedding its own values and belief systems into your mind through continuous repetition and reinforcement. Therefore, the most powerful belief system (right or wrong depends on your circumstances) that started to overpower your thinking was about your self-image and the way you look at the world. For example, if you were born and brought up in a safe and stable home, then you probably grew up seeing the world as a safe and welcoming place. But if someone comes from a chaotic or broken home, seeing all sorts of negative things like abuse, lying, or crimes, then your perception of the world would be as an unsafe, disturbing, and dishonest place.

You could classify these beliefs as fortunate or unfortunate, depending upon how your life shows up currently. Your current life is the result of the actions you have taken so far, and those actions have emanated solely from the mental loops you have formed from so many years. This is because your beliefs define your actions, which in turn define your life. The simple formula works like this:

Mental loops > Beliefs > Actions > Results (your current life)

Unfortunately, the wrong thinking patterns or belief systems become such an integral part of the way you live that you can't see or distinguish them yourself; they become like invisible bugs in your mind.

To understand how your behavior or decisions of everyday life are almost put on autopilot due to these bugs, you need to take help from some magnifying lenses. These magnifying lenses will help you to see these bugs explicitly. Once you see them, understand them, and analyze how your actions have always been influenced by these bugs, you can debug your mind. Only after you have debugged your system from these viruses would you be able to rewire and install the new software or application in your mind.

These magnifying lenses are the mental models, which help you see your mechanical, preset, and automated behavior and give you an instant tool to think differently and make better decisions. If you don't know, mental models are very frequently used by investor Warren Buffett and his billionaire partner, Charlie Munger, to give a direction to their thinking and avoid being swayed by the preset patterns of the mind.

The mental models will unravel how you operate your life with so many preconceived notions about different things in your life. Once you see through them, you'll have a better understanding of how life operates. Mental models are a way to enhance your cognitive abilities, so you could make more intelligent and strategic decisions.

Below are a few of our non-resourceful and limiting thinking patterns, which act as bugs to our mind, and also the ways to get rid of them through the laser rays of mental models.

Confirmation Bias

Confirmation bias is our general tendency to interpret the new evidence as a confirmation of our existing belief system. We are so glued to our old beliefs that instead of learning something new or different, we cherry-pick the information that confirms our existing belief system.

Warren Buffet puts it very aptly when he said: "What the human being is best at doing is interpreting all new information so that their prior conclusions remain intact."

One of the world's best-known skeptics and critical thinkers, Michael Shermer, author of *The Believing Brain: From Spiritual Faiths to Political Convictions—How We*

Construct Beliefs and Reinforce Them as Truths, has explored the reasoning of why people believe anything at all. He bluntly puts it,

"We form our beliefs for a variety of subjective, personal, emotional, and psychological reasons in the context of environments created by family, friends, colleagues, culture, and society at large; after forming our beliefs we then defend, justify, and rationalize them with a host of intellectual reasons, cogent arguments, and rational explanations. Beliefs come first, explanations for beliefs follow."

What a rigid world view, isn't it?

With this approach, it is never possible to look at situations from a different perspective. You are always looking for things to just confirm your existing beliefs. The complexity of confirmation bias arises partly from the fact that it is impossible to overcome it without an awareness of the concept. Even if you are shown evidence to contradict a biased view, you may still interpret it in a manner that reinforces our current perspective.

Let's try to understand this with the help of an example. Due to religious beliefs, in a country like India, even non-vegetarian people consider it a taboo to eat cow's meat, i.e., beef, because they think a cow's life is as precious just as next to humans. However, such people don't mind eating chicken, mutton, pork or other kind of meat. Now if you ask someone from western country, you will get an entirely different perspective. They think that killing a cow will meet the requirement of meat for more meat-eaters as compared to killing a chicken. That is, they say, if you count the number of lives taken for meeting human's meat requirement, it's better to kill one big animal instead of many small chickens. I'm personally not in favor or against any of these ideas. But the point is whatever belief you have, you will find the arguments to support that belief. Thanks to this confirmation bias, you often ignore the other side's perspective, even if there is something new or valuable there, and only choose such information that supports your previous beliefs.

How can you debug your mind from this confirmation bias?

You need to start developing a flexible approach and openness to listen to any divergent thoughts. It's quite possible to change your approach if you start putting yourself in such situations where you get to see different perspectives. Unless you are able to get into the shoes of the other person, until you understand the circumstances responsible for another person's beliefs, you wouldn't question your existing beliefs.

Don't run in the race of being right; it's more important to be in the right race. Don't always be out there to protect your ideas; rather be open and willing to consume new ideas from other people.

Getting rid of confirmation bias requires trying new things, meeting new people, visiting different places, etc. The best way to do this is to pick some topic of interest, which you have some existing knowledge, but you want to explore it further. The next step is to pick some documentary or book by different experts on this topic. Listen, watch, or read about these people explaining their point of view. In this process, you'll find yourself introspecting and also will realize that you often find arguments that support your belief. But here, you have to practice overcoming your desire to just support your beliefs and start to dig deeper to understand the *right and just perspective* that can withstand the test of objectivity.

Availability Heuristics

Heuristics enables a person to discover or learn something for themselves. They are the mental shortcuts that ease the cognitive load of making a decision. We follow heuristics to make decisions faster based on some rules framed for certain situations. Few examples of heuristics could be using a rule of thumb, educated guess, intuitive judgment, guesstimate, stereotyping, profiling, common sense, etc.

Availability heuristic indicates that we make our decisions mostly based on the recency of the events. We often misjudge the frequency and magnitude of the events that have happened recently because of the limitation of our memory. Also, we remember those things better when they have come in a vivid narrative.

According to Harvard professor Max Bazerman, managers conducting performance appraisals often fall victim to the availability heuristic. The recency of events plays a vital role in performance appraisals. Managers give more weight to performance during the three months prior to the evaluation than to the previous nine months of the evaluation period because the recent instances dominate their memory. Also, vivid instances of an employee's behavior (either positive or negative) will be most easily recalled from memory and will appear more numerous than commonplace incidents. These will therefore be weighted more heavily in the performance appraisals.

The availability heuristics is influenced by the ease of recall or retrievability of information of some event. Ease of recall suggests that if something is more easily recalled in your memory, you think that it must occur with a high probability. A study by Karlsson, Loewenstein, and Ariely (2008) showed that people are more likely to purchase insurance to protect themselves after a natural disaster they have just experienced than they are to purchase insurance on this type of disaster before it happens. Their decisions are influenced by the recency of events and retrievability of the information.

Take another example of availability heuristics. It's a fact that strokes cause many more deaths than accidents by road or otherwise, but one study confirmed that 80% of the respondents in the study stated that accidental death is more likely the cause of death. This is because accidental deaths are reported more often in media and present a vivid image and strong impression upon our minds as compared to death from strokes. We remember horrific accidental deaths more clearly and therefore our mind takes immediate judgement based on the recent, more vivid imagery in its records.

Unfortunately, this approach distorts our understanding of the real risks. We often don't do the proper assessment of all the alternatives in front of us and are misguided by ease of recall due to recency of events or retrievability of information in our minds.

How can you debug your mind from availability heuristics?

No doubt, we have to make quicker decisions at times, but we also don't want such promptness that doesn't take into account the real risks involved. The solution is to take a pause before jumping to the conclusion. Don't let emotions or any quick rule of thumb method influence your decision-making in important matters, rather you need to gather proper data, which may take some time.

Availability heuristic supplies you with only the limited information based on your mental ability to easily recall the information depending on the nature of your experience. But you need to go beyond the limited information based on your mental ability to easily recall the information, and look at other relevant data by doing some more research. Only once you have the information that's necessary for making a decision should you make the decision.

At the same time, you shouldn't be sitting over the problem indefinitely on the pretext of researching and collecting more information. Actually, whatever maximum and relevant information you can gather on the subject in the time available to you, you need to do that.

Use the **40-70 Colin Powell Rule** when you are not sure about the adequacy of information available with you. Former U.S. Secretary of State Colin Powell devised this rule about making decisions and coming to a point of action in cases where you lack information. He suggested whenever you want to make some decision on any important aspect, you should have no less than 40% and no more than 70% of the information required for that decision. He states less than 40% of information means we are bound to make wrong decisions. But if we continue to search for more than 70% information, we will end up taking so much time that the decision itself will not deliver any meaningful results, because it's already too late.

Therefore, don't make decisions based on this shortcut of availability heuristic, and do your research to get requisite information before you make any decision.

Hanlon's Razor

Don't you feel sometimes that the whole world is against you? If something awful happens to you, you get a feeling that the world is not being fair to you or there is some conspiracy going against you.

For example, if your manager is not able to give you time for discussion, you start thinking he doesn't like you, so you get scared that you won't receive a good appraisal this year. Or if you don't get a message from your friend for two days in a row, you imagine he or she is not interested in you anymore. If the internet is not working in the cafe, you tend to think that you were cheated by the staff by hanging a board outside saying "free internet" merely to bring you into their shop.

But most of the time, these assumptions are just false stories only created by our own mind. It might be the case that your boss was super busy in some high priority assignment and was worried about his or her career, due to which he couldn't attend the meeting with you. Or your friend might have been travelling on an important trip and due to bad and infrequent network availability, he or she couldn't message you. Or there might have been some technical error in the servers of the internet service provider, which could have tripped off the internet availability at the cafe.

There could be many genuine reasons behind things happening around you, but it is the human tendency to assign malice to any activity, which could be due to simple neglect or innocent mistake. This happens because our minds have a natural tendency to think negatively in the first instance. Psychologists call this "negativity bias." This negativity bias was the reason humans could survive in the early days, living in forests or in dark caves and hunting animals for food. Living in the forest, humans were consistently in the danger of being hunted and eaten by other wild animals. Any movement or sound in the jungle could be a threat to humans. In order to keep alert of all the dangers, our brain has an almond-sized organ called the amygdala. Also known as the fear center of our brain, it is responsible for giving directions to our body to either fight, flight, or freeze. Therefore, our immediate and the first reaction to any situation is that there must be danger out there.

Fortunately, if you are reading this book on your electronic device, it means you are not staying in any dangerous forest. It proves that you have access to internet, credit card, smartphone, and therefore living in a much safer environment. Most of the population is not subject to those dangers today, as they were in the primitive age, thanks to technological developments and massive urbanization. But the unfortunate part is that our brain's amygdala still perceives any kind of fear as a life or death situation, which is no more the case in reality. Instead of telling our mind that there can be a genuine reason behind what happened, we get carried away by the negativity and start thinking adversely about any situation.

How can you overcome this malice-assigning tendency?

You can overcome this by using Hanlon's Razor Theory, which is a very effective mental model that states: Never attribute to malice that which can be adequately explained by neglect.

The phrase "Hanlon's razor" was coined by Robert J. Hanlon, but it has been voiced by many people throughout history. Napoleon Bonaparte also famously declared: "Never ascribe to malice that which is adequately explained by incompetence."

Goethe wrote similarly in *The Sorrows of Young Werther* in 1774:

"Misunderstandings and neglect create more confusion in this world than trickery and malice. At any rate, the last two are certainly much less frequent."

Hanlon's razor can help you in situations when you deal with people, institutions, or entities you don't like. In such situations, your natural tendency is to assume those people have bad intentions toward you. Even their neutral behavior or actions might seem rude or aggressive to you.

When such people make a mistake, you'd never react with empathy or understanding toward that person.

Here, it's important to apply Hanlon's razor, because this theory will help you to put your preconceived notions aside and assess the other side's behavior with a clear and neutral mindset. Applying Hanlon's razor in our day-to-day lives allows us to better develop relationships, become less judgmental, and improve rationality. **Hanlon's razor allows us to give people the benefit of the doubt and have more empathy.**

Hanlon's razor can be utilized in most of the situations as a rule of thumb, however like with everything there are exceptions to this rule. If you have empirical evidence or information that supports the malice on the part of the other side, then you need to be careful dealing with such a person. For example, if someone is coming toward you with a knife in his hands, this rule doesn't apply. Here, you need to listen to your amygdala's instructions and be prepared to handle the situation.

Halo Effect

The halo effect is the human tendency to oversimplify the things without getting the necessary details and make decisions based on initial impressions. This is the phenomenon where, if you like someone due to a particular trait, you tend to believe that the person has other qualities also.

The word "halo" means a circle of light shown around the body or head of a saint or a holy person to show their holiness. In psychological terms, halo effect means that you make an overall perception of someone based on your judgement of the person on one factor. It generally happens if you like someone, then start to assume that the person possessing multiple characteristics and traits to handle other things as well.

Psychologist Edward Thorndike first coined this term "halo effect." In the experiment described in his research papers, Thorndike asked commanding officers in the military to evaluate a variety of qualities in their subordinate soldiers. These characteristics included such things as leadership, physical appearance, intelligence, loyalty, and dependability. The goal of this experiment was to determine how ratings of one quality bled over to assessments of other characteristics. He found that high ratings of a particular quality correlated to high ratings of other characteristics, while negative ratings of a specific quality also led to lower ratings of other characteristics.

Practical observations of the halo effect are visible across many situations. For example, a teacher in the classroom can be subject to halo effect in rating a well-behaved student as an intelligent, diligent, and smart person. In this example, halo effect affects the students' overall rating and in some cases also affect the students' grade. Similarly, in corporate world, during employees' performance appraisals, the subordinates, who appear to follow the direction of his or her manager enthusiastically gets the benefit of the halo effect from their manager. In fact, the halo effect is probably the most common bias in performance appraisals. The supervisor may give prominence to a single characteristic of the employee, such as enthusiasm, and allow the entire evaluation to be colored by how he or she judges the employee on that one characteristic. That's why we hear the term blue-eyed-guy or gal, if some manager pays more attention or listens more to some subordinate due to a few traits of latter.

Therefore, the halo affect is misguiding you and not helping you to make the right decision based on the holistic parameters.

What Should You Do to Avoid the Halo Effect?

The right approach to counter the halo effect is to follow the objective approach. To be specific, you need to list out all the necessary parameters for arriving at a decision. Then you need to assign weight to each parameter by assigning a specific number from 1 to 10—1 for least weight and 10 for maximum weight. Once done, you can make a total of all the parameters for specific alternatives and then decide.

For example, suppose you have to hire an employee out of three candidates A, B, and C. Here, you need to specifically list out the necessary soft skills and job skills necessary to perform the job. Your parameters can be qualifications, years of experience, industry work, confidence level, enthusiasm, the desire to learn, etc. If you are not careful enough, the halo effect will start influencing your decision, because you might like one candidate over the other due to his attractiveness, communication skills, etc, which will tend to color your impression on other traits too. That's where being objective and giving weight to different parameters safeguard you from this biased approach germinating out of the halo effect.

To sum up, the above mental models will prompt you to challenge your existing thinking patterns. You'll often find yourself nudging yourself to think differently. Next time, if your spouse spills water on your shirt while you are getting ready for some friend's cocktail party, you won't get angry and think negatively about her , because you can now use Hanlon's razor to not assign malice to his or her behavior. Similarly, you won't be unnecessarily looking for evidence just to validate your old beliefs at the cost of not gaining new knowledge or perspective.

Precisely, once you start implementing these mental models practically in your life (and trust me, you will have plenty of instances to apply them), you will start debugging your mind from the unsupportive beliefs and perceptions that are not serving your anymore.

Let's now move to the next section, where you will learn about the groundwork necessary to prime your mind to prepare it for your mind hacking journey.

Chapter 5: Groundwork for Fertile Mind

****

"Create the highest, grandest vision possible for your life, because you become what you believe."

– Oprah Winfrey

OK, so far we have discussed what the mind is and how it operates. We talked about what we mean by hacking your mind and also about bugs that adversely affect our decisions and what we should do about them. From here onwards, we will shift gears. In this chapter, you will learn few important preparatory steps that will later speed up your mind hacking journey.

Let's dive straight into these strategies:

Priming

Priming is a technique used in psychology whereby exposure to a particular stimulus influences a response to a subsequent stimulus without any conscious guidance or attention. The dictionary meaning of priming is "to tell someone something that will prepare them for a particular situation."

Priming requires you to expose your mind to certain things, events or patterns, so that it behaves in a particular desired way. Let me give you a small example of how priming works.

Read the word "**SO_P**." In this word, you need to fill in the gap. Different letters might come into your mind to give a word. Now here is how priming work.

If you are exposed to the word "eat" or "drink," or if you are sitting at the dining table or at some restaurant before the above fill-in-the-blank quiz, the immediate response that could come up in your mind might be "**SOUP**." But now take a different situation. If you are shown the word "shower" or "bath" or you're doing your morning routine activities, then the immediate word that comes to your mind will be "**SOAP**."

This is what priming does. We're primed when exposure to a particular word or situation causes us to summon related words or concepts.

Priming is a simple technique because all it involves is talking to yourself in a particular way; it involves reciting a given set of words that are designed to alter your mindset. No, it's not brainwashing and it cannot make you do anything you don't want to do. What it can accomplish, however, is putting you into a state of mind that will be more useful to you with a given situation or task.

There was a study conducted by the researchers at Yale University. As a part of study, in the elevator on the way to the lab, a member of the study team would casually ask the participant to hold their coffee. The team member would then write down some information about the participant, then get their coffee back. Each participant would hold the cup of coffee for somewhere between 10 and 25 seconds. For half the participants the coffee was hot, while the other half held cold cups of coffee. That was the only difference between the two groups of participants.

Each of the participants who held the coffee cup for that shorter duration asked to give some brief description of the team member. They all gave the same physical description of the member. But here comes the interesting observation: now the participants were asked about their personality traits. The participants who'd held the hot coffee for a few seconds rated the person has generous, happy, and more social than those who'd held cold cup. The people who'd held cold cups were more likely to judge that the study member was unhappy, selfish, and irritable.

Notice that there was no difference in the physical appearance of the study member in those 10 to 25 seconds of interaction. But still the participants tested the study member differently on the personality traits. The researcher noted that merely by holding a hot cup or cold cup for a few seconds did the work of priming the minds of the participants, which prompted them to observe the study member differently.

Now let me give some breaking news here.

You are already priming yourself for hacking your mind in the course of your reading so far.

How?

Remember the analogy of a computer in reference to your mind? Hacking is a concept more common to getting access to the hidden codes of computer software and then using or altering it to your advantage. You compared your mind to a computer software. Then we also discussed that if you want to be a hacker, you should have access to the admin rights and not just as a "regular user," meaning that you should have all administration rights to make all the changes to help you reprogram.

Also, your mind was compared to a movie running in your head, with the objective to disassociate you from your mind, because only if something is separate from you can you can think of controlling it. Since the beginning, you were being primed that your mind was some different object other than you. It's something that can be reprogrammed like computer software.

Therefore, you can see priming as using some concept that triggers you to take desired actions. With all the above analogies and illustrations, you have primed yourself to believe that your mind can be altered or reprogrammed like software.

How should you use priming going forward?

The approach is simple. Whatever you want to learn or achieve as your goal, you need to start communicating similar words or situations to your mind.

To help you, I will give another example. Let me assume that you have some picture in your mind of a dream house, a big car, or some trip you'd like to take. As you think of your dream, you get an instant impulse in your mind to perform better and earn more money sooner, and to obtain your dream possessions or experience. That's the objective behind vision boards (with pictures of all your dream objects pasted on it) or self-affirmations, because they constantly prime you to behave in a particular way.

Priming is all about using some stimulus that directs your mind to the desired objective. Whatever goal you want to achieve, you need to keep priming your mind by presenting the objects or thoughts that immediately direct your attention to the goal. There are many ways in which you can prime your mind for success. A few of them include:

- Reading great personal development books
- Meeting personally or listening to great people using podcasts or Youtube videos. Reading biographies of legends.
- Surrounding yourself with inspirational quotes (I personally have posted two pages of inspirational quotes, thoughtfully curated, for my personal needs to keep me on my track.)
- Researching and keep learning newer and more effective ways to carry out your tasks
- Building your vision board, as explained above

When you expose yourself to the above activities, they will act as stimuli to let you think about constantly improving yourself. But remember, this is not a once-a-week kind of activity, rather you have to do it regularly.

Jim Rohn said once: "People often say that motivation doesn't last. Well, neither does bathing—that's why we recommend it daily."

I liked Tony Robbins's 10-minute morning priming routine with 8 steps to make you ready for success available at https://www.tonyrobbins.com/ask-tony/priming/, and this will show you a good example of what priming looks like.

The 5 Whys Principle

Children naturally follow this principle very well. You might have already observed that young children have a tendency to keep asking *why* certain things happen the way they happen. They have innate curiosity to know the reason behind certain things. In fact, this desire to ask question is what enhances their knowledge of the world in those initial years.

Actually, this questioning technique is a very important part of the Six Sigma System, which is a quality control system with a detailed methodology for eliminating defects in any process or service, and mainly used in manufacturing processes. By repeatedly asking *why* (and five is stated as good rule of thumb), you can easily peel the layers off the surface level that can lead to the root cause of any problem.

The originator of this "5 Why" principle was Sakichi Toyoda, a Japanese gentleman, who later on found Toyota Motor Corporation, the world's leading automobile manufacturing corporation. Born in 1867, Toyoda realized in his youth that most Japanese textile factories used wooden looms to produce cloth, which was a highly labor-oriented, slow, and mundane job, and also the quality of the work was not good. After experimenting, he invented a power loom that could work with steam and this tremendously improved the quality and pace of manufacturing textile and saved tons of time in manufacturing. Later on, Toyoda made some further improvements and invented fully automated power looms, which were much faster and further enhanced the manufacturing capacity.

While Toyoda was a genius in inventing new technology, he was equally focused in innovating ways to improve the process of manufacturing. His main belief in the manufacturing process was that it was not always the people who failed, rather it was process that failed.

In his quest to solve process-related problems, he invented the technique of the "5 Whys" to track the problem to the root cause. Whenever there was a lapse or system failure, he continued to ask the concerned employee the "reason" five times to get to the root cause of the problem.

You can try this 5 Why technique in your own life. For example, if you are not able to deliver your best output at your workplace, you can start asking the "5 Whys" to get to the reason. Your reasons may start like this:

1. You always feel anxious about committing a mistake in your work.

Ask *why* it is so?

2. Your manager might have scolded you about your quality, which has aggravated your anxiety over the work.

Now ask *why* did your boss scold you in first place?

3. The reason might be that there was a new technology or system that required enough learning before you could implement it in your work, and you couldn't update your knowledge.

Again, ask *why* you failed to learn this new technology?

4. The reason might be that you had some family problem going on that was stealing your attention from work, and you could not focus on your work.

Here is another *why* you should ask. What was the reason for your family problems?

5. You realized that there was some disconnect on some aspect of your relationship with your partner in the

back of your mind, and it was affecting your work behavior.

The core reason behind your inability to deliver the results at your office was some family problem, which on the surface level appeared to be just anxiety and fear from your boss's scolding.

Just remember, asking 5 whys is not a hard-and-fast rule, rather it's arbitrary. The idea is to go deeper until the last layer of the problem, until you see the root cause. Therefore, you may have to ask four, six, or seven whys before you can unravel the core issue of any problem. The important point is to stop asking why when the useful response stop coming further.

The 5 Whys approach works well in troubleshooting, quality improvement, and general problem solving. You need to awaken your childhood curiosity and dig deeper to find the real reason behind any problem.

Hacking your mind requires you to uncover the connections between different loops in your mind's software. Only after you know the real cause can you set yourself up to find the permanent solution to your problems.

To summarize, you need to start creating such an environment where you build such habits that prime your mind toward looking for the ways to improve your mental faculties. Also, it's important to develop the habits of inquisitiveness and go to the root cause of problem, because this will prevent you from being stuck in addressing the surface level symptoms and save you time.

The focus of the previous and the current chapter was to open up your mind to the newer ways of looking around and to free up your mind, so you can focus on sharpening your mental faculties.

You can't let life happen to you unconsciously; rather you have to take charge of the situation. Therefore, in the next chapter onward, you will learn the core strategies to unlock your mind's hidden and massive potential. The first one is all about mastering your attention, which you will learn in the following chapter.

Chapter 6: Attention - Your Psychic Ability: How to Master It?

****

> *"Concentrate all your thoughts upon the work at hand. The sun's rays do not burn until brought to a focus."*
>
> *- Alexander Graham Bell*

The attention span of modern man has been dramatically reduced, thanks to the advent of addictive technology. The immediate attention span (one single block of concentration) of a goldfish that is notorious for its lack of focusing capacity is nine seconds and ironically humans' immediate attention span has reduced even lower than attention-starved goldfish.

A recent study[6] conducted by Microsoft Corporation revealed that humans lose their attention about every eight seconds. In this study, the researchers studied the brain activities of participants using electroencephelograms (EEGs) and found that since the year 2000 (around the time mobile technology was invented), the average attention span has dropped from twelve seconds to around eight seconds.

Your attention is the most precious asset you have in this modern economy, where everyone is running to steal your attention. Big companies are spending billions of dollars on advertisements to grab your attention to the advertisement of their products. They are consistently out to distract you to buy their products or services. It makes our focus all the more vulnerable to the things really important to live a meaningful life.

William James, a psychologist, once said, "voluntarily bringing back a wandering attention, over and over again, is the very root of judgment, character, and will. An education which should improve this

[6] https://www.medicaldaily.com/human-attention-span-shortens-8-seconds-due-digital-technology-3-ways-stay-focused-333474

faculty would be the education par excellence."

In his book, *Flow: The Psychology Of Optimal Experience*, Mihaly Csikszentmihalyi explains that attention is the psychic energy. He states that the mark of a person who is in control of his consciousness has the ability to focus attention at will, to be oblivious to distractions, and to concentrate as long as it takes to achieve a goal. Similarly, Theron Q. Dumont in *The Power of Concentration* talks highly about the significance of attention in the words below:

"The rays of the sun, when focused upon an object by means of a sun glass, produce a heat many times greater than the scattered rays of the same source of light and heat. This is true of attention. Scatter it and you get but ordinary results. But center it upon one thing and you secure much better results. When you focus your attention upon an object your every action, voluntary and involuntary, is in the direction of attaining that object. If you will focus your energies upon a thing to the exclusion of everything else, you generate the force that can bring you what you want."

Also Mark Victor Hansen puts is so succinctly in below words:

> *"Focused mind power is one of the strongest forces on earth."*

You must have realized the significance of mastering your attention because it has the potential to make you see things, which you can never see if you're constantly distracted. So here is the most important question to be addressed:

How can we achieve laser-sharp focus and become masters of our attention?

John Hargrave holistically explains how you can look at your attention in two different ways. The first one is your "voluntary" or "top-down" attention. Here, you choose to direct your mind to a particular task or activity. The other kind of attention is "reflexive" or "bottom-up." It is when something catches your attention suddenly, without any effort on your part. If someone calls a name in a crowd that rhymes with your name, then immediately your mind gets directed toward the source of that voice.

The challenge of modern man is two-fold. You need to strengthen your "top-down" attention (your ability to concentrate) as well as weaken your "bottom-up" attention (the uncontrolled tendency to get distracted). Therefore, in order to strengthen your concentration abilities, you need to focus on two activities simultaneously: (1) reclaiming your attention through reducing the distractions and (2) retraining your mind through concentration exercise.

1. Get Rid of Distractions to Reclaim Your Attention

How do you reclaim your attention by reducing distraction?

A real-life instance from an event known as Extreme Memory Tournament (XMT), which first happened at San Diego[7] will give you clarity about the ways to reclaim your attention. XMT is a fast-paced, digitally

[7]

https://well.blogs.nytimes.com/2014/05/19/rememberi
ng-as-an-extreme-sport/

enhanced memory contest, where sixteen participants from all over the world participated in that first event. These participants, also known as "memory athletes" stare consistently at computer screens that rapidly flash numbers, names, or images. They need to memorize the information displayed on the screen and restate the information from their memory with pinpoint accuracy. Whoever can recollect the information most accurately and in the fastest way wins the competition.

Out of these sixteen participants, one participant from Norway named Ola Kare Risa had a unique way to shut out any distractions. He wore noise-cancelling headphones to avoid any disturbance. Additionally, he wore a cap that had a long visor and side flaps. The cap with a long visor and side flaps was made so that he could only see the computer screen and nothing else in order to kill the chances of any distractions from his side. It looked similar to the way horses wear blinders, so they could focus only on the front. You can realize the efforts made by this man to kill the possibility of any kind of distraction to weaken the reflexive or bottom-up attention.

I'm not suggesting you to wear the outfits or take precautions like this guy from Norway, as your environment may not permit you to remain so secluded if you work a day job that involves working as a part of team. But the idea was to show you an example of how these memory athletes made efforts to kill their distraction. Therefore, to tap the full potential of your mind, you also need to remove the amount of distractions that come in your way. These distractions can pop up in many shapes and forms, and, at times, when you need to focus on your most important work.

Since this section is about preparing yourself before you hack your mind's full potential, you need to work on your environment to remove distractions.

How do you do it?

Here are a few simple ways to remove distractions from your day-to-day life:

- ***Allocate specific times*** for social media during the day and then put all your notifications on silent mode.

This is because social media beeps and notification keeps buzzing every minute or so, and that tempts you to check that out. This is because these notifications have an element of surprise or uncertainty in them and our brain releases a happy chemical called dopamine, if there is some element of novelty. But this tendency to get distracted every few minutes keeps you always distracted and seriously hampers your concentration abilities.

- ***Email distractions***: For some people, it might not sound feasible and they might say that they need to check emails and respond immediately. But even here, you can try to put your emails on silent mode with the exception of few important people, whose messages you need to address immediately. For others, restrict yourself to watch these emails only during those allocated hours. Try to reduce the frequency of checking your email to a minimum.

- **_Internet distractions_**: Not only social media, but internet addiction is also another source of distraction. You might want to check some statistics related to your business frequently. Or you may want to check out some news at times. But these are all excuses your mind makes to get away from important work (which often requires you to put in long concentrated hours). Also allocate a dedicated time-slot for such distractions.

- **_Clean your desk_**: Just have a quick look at your workstation. Is it clumsy and scattered or is it organized? If the surrounding environment around you is scattered, that will affect the concentration ability of your mind, as the scattered things will divert your attention from the work you are doing.

In a study[8] conducted by Boyoun (Grace) Chae and Rui (Juliet) Zhu,

---

[8] https://hbr.org/2015/01/why-a-messy-workspace-

100 undergraduates were exposed to one of two environments. The first was a cluttered office with cups and boxes strewn around. The other was a neat and tidy desk. After exposure, the students were asked to do a task that was described to them as "challenging"—but in reality, the task was unsolvable. The results showed that the students exposed to the neat office stuck with the problem for an average of 18 minutes, compared to the ones who saw the messy desk, could only focus for about 11 minutes on average.

Therefore, removing distractions means getting rid of any kind of clutter that can take away your attention.

- *Use ABC Steps:* This trick of the ABC method was recommended by experts at Harvard Business Review when it comes to getting rid of distraction and maintaining your focus on the thing at hand. The ABC

undermines-your-persistence

method is like using your brain's brake pedal.

It works like this: Whenever you are in the middle of important work and there is something coming to hijack your attention, apply the ABC formula described below:

- A: Be **Aware** of the options in front of you.

- B: **Breathe** deeply and consider your options.

- C: **Choose** thoughtfully after considering your main goals. If the new thing that popped up during your important work helps you to progress on the important work, accept it. If not, then choose to assign lower priority to the new thing, after your important work.

2. Concentration Tricks To Retrain Your Mind

Now let's talk about the second important aspect of attention, namely voluntary or top-bottom attention by way of learning techniques to redirecting your mind to a particular task or activity.

Concentration tricks are nothing but some mental games that focus on concentrating your mind on a particular thing. The focus point could be anything and the simplest is your breath. It would sound similar to meditation or mindfulness practice, but here the objective of doing this is a mental exercise (just like how you stress your physical muscles to build strength) entirely to increase the attention capacity. That's why Hargrave preferred to give them the name of concentration tricks and not meditation. The more you are able to direct your attention on any particular thing, the sooner and better you will develop the abilities to hack your mind.

The basic concentration trick involves sitting for a period of say twenty minutes. You may start with five minutes, and then gradually increase it to ten and then twenty minutes. In this short period of sitting quietly, you need to focus on your breath consistently. The game is to keep observing how many times you got distracted from your breath. Whenever you notice that your thoughts swayed in your mind, just count that instance and give yourself a score of +1. Keep doing this for the entire period. When you find yourself lost in thoughts and redirect to your breath, this itself means strengthening your attention muscle. If you caught your mind wandering twenty times on your first try, later on you may find that the instances reduced to ten, which is a winning score for you.

These concentration games can be made easier, more interesting and exciting by offering it in different variants. But the key recommendation here is to decide in advance what variant you will be using during the entire concentration practice. You will notice that your mind will want to change the variant in between the concentration practice, but please realize that this is the mind's trick to get distracted from what it was intended to focus on. Therefore, choose the trick and stick to it. Here are few variants of the concentration technique suggested by Hargrave that I found quite intriguing (especially the second bullet below):

- ***The Illuminati***: Instead of focusing on the nostrils, focus on the point between the eyebrows.
- ***Alien Blaster***: Pretend each thought is an alien. Focus on your breath while remaining vigilant for stray aliens breaking through your defense shield. Whenever you see a thought arising, mentally say, "thought," which disintegrates the alien with a hydrogen-ion particle blaster.
- ***The Third Nipple***: Instead of focusing on the nostrils, focus on the point between the breasts.
- ***Golden Breath***: Instead of focusing on the nostrils, focus on the air itself as you inhale and exhale. Imagine that you are taking in pure oxygen, a delicious smell, or a healing elixir.

The better you perform on the concentration games, the sooner you will improve your attention capacity, which in turn will improve your mental faculties to see your goal clearly and make better decisions.

What about multitasking?

Some people who are strong proponents of multitasking—who think that handling multiple tasks simultaneously gets more things done in less time—would need some evidence to prove otherwise. And thanks to enough scientific research, it can be stated that multitasking is in fact a myth.

Studies have shown that you're slower when you switch between tasks than when you do one task repeatedly—and that you grow less and less efficient as the tasks grow increasingly complex. According to the late Stanford neuroscientist Clifford Nass[9], multitasking should really be called "multi-switching," because the human brain does not have the capacity to focus on several tasks at once. If you are multitasking, you are simply switching back and forth between tasks very quickly, which almost always results in a loss of productivity.

Nass States, "People who multitask all the time can't filter out irrelevancy. They can't manage a working memory. They're

---

[9] http://www.npr.org/2013/05/10/182861382/the-myth-of-multitasking

chronically distracted. They're even terrible at multitasking. When we ask them to multitask, they're actually worse at it. So they're pretty much mental wrecks."

There is also a concept of attention residue, as stated by Cal Newport in his bestselling book *Deep Work*. The research has identified that when you try to switch between different activities frequently, your attention doesn't immediately follow. This is because a residue of your attention remains stuck thinking about the original task. Due to this attention residue in the original task, people demonstrate poor performance in the next activity. More intense the residue —worse the performance.

Newport further advises that to produce at your peak level, you need to work for extended periods with full concentration on a single task free from distraction. Put another way, the type of work that optimizes performance is deep work. The formula for high quality work as suggested by Newport works like this: *High Quality Work Produced = Time Spent X Intensity of Focus.*

It is the intensity of focus on an important task for longer periods that determines the quality of your work, and not the jumping between different task together.

Therefore, one can conclude that to harness the maximum potential of your mind, it's very important to develop your focus muscles. The two-fold approach of reclaiming your attention by getting rid of distractions and using concentration tricks to retrain your mind serve a dual purpose: Firstly, you won't be affected by distractions, and secondly, you build your attention by training your mind to focus on one thing for longer.

Now let's move on to the next chapter to understand other mental work necessary to gain momentum by involving your subconscious mind in the game.

Chapter 7: Mental Techniques to Tap Your Sub-conscious Mind

****

"If you can't conceive of things that don't exist, you can't create anything new. If you can't dream up worlds that might be, then you are limited to the worlds other people describe."

- Robert and Michele Root-Bernstein

Imagination is more important than knowledge.

The above seems like a very bold statement, doesn't it? Some highly rational, logical, or practical thinking people would probably throw this idea out of the window.

But no, this is not merely a rhetoric statement. It was the life experience of the legend Albert Einstein, the genius and Nobel prize winner, who developed his award-winning theories primarily through the power of imagination.

Surprisingly, Einstein was not one of the best learners in history. His earlier schools experience and his patent office job demonstrated that. In fact, his school teacher was so frustrated with his behavior that he went to the extent of making the statement, "Nothing will ever become of you." Moreover the fact that he was stuck in his low-level government job as a third-class patent clerk doesn't speak highly about his knowledge.

But the best part of his government job stint was that it gave him a plenty of time to imagine different ideas that other people might consider silly. He used to write his ideas or wild thoughts on paper and stored them in one his drawers. His philosophy was to stay open to any kind of thought his imagination took him to, like what would it feel like if you were sitting on a beam of light and travelling on that?

He called his thoughts and ideas stored in his drawer as the "department of theoretical physics."[10] But Einstein's award-winning theories or ideas didn't happen in some lab or by performing physical examples, rather it all started by experimenting in his own mind. He gives credit of all his award-winning abilities to the power of his imagination and believed that *imagination was rather a very high-end thinking process.* He was deeply convinced about the power of imagination, which is clearly evident when he said:

"Imagination is more important than knowledge. ***For knowledge is limited, whereas imagination embraces the entire world, stimulating progress, giving birth to evolution.****"*

Einstein was the living example of a genius, who hacked the potential of his mind to the highest level: through the power of his creative imagination. Anyone sincere about knowing and extracting more out of his mind can never afford to underestimate the significance of imagination.

10

https://www.salon.com/2014/02/16/einstein_the_failure_how_historys_greatest_physicist_flirted_with_disaster/

To hack the mind's creative abilities to the fullest, it's important to learn and nurture this important cognitive process of our minds. Let's start by understanding what exactly is imagination and then we will talk about how you can develop your imagination.

As per Dictionary definition, "imagination as the act or power of forming a mental image of something not present to the senses or never before wholly perceived in reality."

It means with the power of imagination, you create something entirely in your own mind with a fusion of multiple ideas and coming out with some different and non-existent concept. You can choose whatever you want to imagine. It's your own mind that draws inferences from different situations and imagines as it wants to. You can train your mind to choose imagination to get the results you want in your life.

The power of the human mind to imagine is infinite; it's a vastly unexplored field. There is no limit to what you can imagine. You can go as crazy as you want in your imagination. To give you some food for thought, I am imagining right now that Earth and other planets in the solar system are moving out of their orbit (around the sun) and are now revolving around the moon. Though it won't ever happen (or maybe it will happen someday; who knows the universe's plans), the point is that you can imagine anything in your mind.

Anyway, the above was just an example to illustrate that it's not that you have to get some training or attend a course to start imagining. You have the ability to imagine anything and anywhere. But here is the thing: Don't take it lightly, because your imagination doesn't remain merely at the imagination level, it can come out in the real world itself and there are studies that demonstrate the power of imagination.

In fact, an experiment was conducted by Ellen Langer, a professor of psychology at Harvard, in 1979 to test the power of imagination on the physical health of the people who participated in the experiment, as she explains in her book *Counterclockwise*.

In the experiment, the researchers created an environment that looked and felt exactly like the late 1950s. They took care of every minute detail—the songs playing in the background, black and white television, old-fashioned radio, magazines of that period, etc. The eight participants, in their 70s, were required to live in this environment as if they were young.

When the subjects entered into this virtual reality world, they were told not only to reminisce about their younger self, but also to attempt to psychologically behave as if they were young people of 1959. The idea they were sold upon was that if they successfully attempted this, they would start feeling as if they were in the 1950s.

These older people, following the instructions, acted as if they were young people. They were encouraged to talk in the present tense as young people. There was no mirror, no current images or anything that could spoil the illusion of being young.

The experiment was successfully completed and the results were terrific. These people were now tested on various age-related parameters—memory, dexterity, general cognitive ability—and there were significant improvements. They were noted as sitting straighter and looking younger than before they entered the virtual room. Also, surprisingly, some people displayed improved vision. As the *New York Times Magazine* reported[11], they "had put their minds in an earlier time, and their bodies went along for the ride."

There are tons of examples where with the power of imagination some people have made extremely impactful inventions to make the live of most people easier.

Another good example of a figure with huge imagination is Jeff Bezos, founder of Amazon, who one fine day thought up of an idea that would make the Amazon shopping experience much smoother for consumers. The idea was to make it possible for people to buy products with one click of a button. You see the "1-click-buy" button on Amazon these days and may find this a pretty simple tool, but Bezos came up with this idea in the late 1990s when the internet had just started and website development involved a ton of technical work. He shared his idea

[11] https://www.businessinsider.in/A-radical-experiment-tried-to-make-old-people-young-again-and-the-results-were-astonishing/articleshow/46831619.cms

with his web-developer, who said that it would take a dozen steps to sell a product with 1-click, like getting the customer to fill out personal details, connecting with the payment processer bank, filling out pin details, etc. The developers said it was extremely difficult to integrate everything and produce a 1-click-buy experience, but Bezos insisted that it would be possible with some technical upgrading and efforts, and he was right. Finally, we have this amazing 1-click-buy button to make for a smoother buying experience due to Amazon's pioneering, which originated from the wild imagination of Jeff Bezos. I personally love this feature and use it every time on Amazon when I have decided to buy a product.

Similarly, had it not been the imagination of Steve Jobs (with the end objective of providing a seamless phone experience to users) to visualize a touch phone, all of us may still be using phones with much more limited functionalities.

Recently Elon Musk, the founder of Paypal, SpaceX, and Tesla Motors, imagined using spaceships to make traveling faster on Earth. We all know rockets were invented to carry spacecrafts into space, but Musk's imagination was altogether on a different spectrum. He presented the idea about using a spaceship, which will start from destination A on Earth, travel into space, (where it will travel much faster since there is no gravity), and then land at destination B on Earth. If this idea works, it could cover the travel between any two locations in the world in less than one hour. You could travel from Shanghai to New York in under 40 minutes.How does that sound for a change? You can see Musk's amazing video here at Travel Everywhere In Earth Within 30 Minutes.[12]

Don't assume that imagination is something that is gifted to only a limited number of people. The problem is our outlook towards the thing. John Hargrave puts it rightly when he says:

> *"We have a strange attitude toward imagination. When we see it in geniuses like Jeff Bezos, we call it 'vision.' When we*

---

[12] https://www.youtube.com/watch?v=-cvRfu7dfCo

see it in children, we call it 'cute.' When we see it in ourselves, we often call it 'a dumb idea' or 'a crazy thought.' In reality, however, it's the same skill: the skill of developing a clear mental picture."

Of course, if you are just starting out, some ideas will sound a bit crazy to you. But here is the thing, every great idea seemed crazy in the beginning. The people in the past who believed that the Earth is flat and was the center of the universe initially thrashed the idea that the Earth was round and not the center of universe. But the world is mostly impacted by the people with the most unconventional thinking. Steve Jobs once rightly put it:

"Those who are crazy enough to think they can change the world usually do."

How do you improve your imagination?

Why people are not able to imagine is because imagination is a really hard work. Here we are talking about actively imagining and creating a clear mental picture of things.

Here are a few tips you can use to build your imagination muscles:

- Imagine the possibility of anything that your mind can conceive of; and then find the ways to support the happening of that possibility.

- Don't ridicule or laugh at any possibility. It's only the limitation of your mind which prompts you to choose thoughts based on known past and stops you to travel into unknown future, because the job of our mind is to ensure your survival. For your mind, everything known is safe, and everything unknown means danger.

For example, you may think of building a hanging house that stays in the air. You can see I am flying too high with the power of imagination. But let's try to come up with the possible ways that you could achieve this. Think about what is needed to make this a reality:

- How would you first ensure that you overcome the force of gravity and ensure the house doesn't get pulled down by the gravity?
- How would you make sure that you don't get lost in space, if you go too high in space?
- How would you ensure that your house doesn't collide with airplanes or spaceships?
- How would you minimize the cost of staying in the hanging house with all your family members, furniture, belongings, etc.?

The idea in above example was not to let your rational mind become a hurdle in order to see what comes to you as a possibility. Once you start putting your mind to these kinds of exercises, you start getting ideas to make them possible.

While the above experiment was a bit stretch of the imagination, let's come to the ground to see if you could imagine something rather easily achievable. How about doubling your salary or income in one year? Again, your inner critic will laugh, but give yourself a challenge and think about it using your imagination. Think about how you can really make it if you don't allow your own limiting thoughts to present obstacles. Below is what you should probably do:

- Examine the outliers in your industry and see if anyone has done it. If so, know their story, learn from them, and engage them as coaches.
- If it is difficult in your field or niche, can you think of learning a new skill that can garner you that ability to double your income?
- Critically examine what your daily activities are and what activities need to be replaced so you get more return on your time invested.

Finally, imagination is the power that enables you to think of a better future. If you can't imagine a future that is better than your past, then you are destined to live the way you have always lived. But if you are not content with your past and present, it's the power of imagination that will help you sow the seeds of possibility in your mind. We can say that imagination has reality. It's real in the same way that a blueprint is real to the skyscraper.

Now let's talk about another helpful tool that will help you visualize your future.

Visualization

You might ask, "We just talked about imagination, then why we are talking about 'visualization'? Aren't they the same?"

To some people, imagination and visualization might appear similar. So it's important to first clarify the difference between imagination and visualization.

Imagination is a general ability to create something in your mind. It's the fundamental requirement for the creativity building block. On the other hand, visualization is more specific; you can call it a *targeted imagination*. You visualize a specific outcome emerging by way of following a specific process. The better the visualization, the more details, more vividness, more imagery and sensory experiences you will have in your mind.

One example of another genius from history will explain this concept better. Nikola Tesla was the greatest geek of his time, who had the great ability to mentally visualize images so clearly, as if they were actually physically present in the world out there. Tesla was a Serbian-American inventor, who was awarded more than 300 patents during his lifetime for his diverse set of inventions, like electric motors, ship navigation devices, wireless lighting, etc. He was the inventor of the modern alternate current (AC) motors. As a perfect example of a mind hacker, Tesla was known for many years to perfect his ideas about creating a device that could project the thoughts running in a human mind onto the wall—an invention, he called "thought camera".

Tesla was gifted with visual thinking skills. If you say a word in front of him, say a motor, he could imagine the entire motor circuitry in his mind. He had developed this ability to run mental visualization or simulations—a detailed picture of exactly what you wanted to achieve—by working through all the problems, obstacles and the complete process in your mind.

This is different than imagination—that's why I said visualization is a targeted imagination. Another way to describe it is imagination is a broad imagery of the final destination, but visualization is a very specific and detailed step and process to reach there.

Walt Disney was also famous for his likings of visualization, and he famously coined a term "imagineering." His idea was to visualize a sensory rich visualization, and this simple technique has proven beneficial to athletes who got their best results due to this technique only. This is because for any kind of performance outside, the mental preparation is as necessary as physical training.

In his book, *The Art of Mental Training*, D. C. Gonzalez shares a story about Pelé, who apparently, was a huge imagineering guy. An hour before every game, Pelé would grab a couple towels and lay down somewhere in the locker room. He'd roll one towel up for a mini-pillow and use the other to cover his eyes. Then he'd go to work in his mental gym.

First, he'd bring to mind images of playing on the beach as a kid—seeing and feeling the love and enthusiasm with which that little version of him ran around the soccer field. Then, he'd imagine some of his best performances, where he demonstrated total mastery. He'd see it. He'd feel it.

At last, he'd imagine THAT day's performance. The enthusiasm and love of his childhood and the mastery of his recent performances melded into an extraordinary performance in his mind for that next game within this 30 minutes of imagineering. That's what he did before every single game. Then he'd walk onto the field and be unstoppable—doing precisely what he had just experienced in his mind.

The important point to remember here is that *you need to focus on your performance and not on the results*. Pelé didn't spend 30 minutes imagining receiving a gold medal or a million dollars check after winning the game. Those are outcomes – rather he focused on what he was going to do - his performance.

Studies to back up the effectiveness of Visualization

There are numerous studies that show when people were asked to imagine a future scenario, then asked about the likelihood of achieving that scenario, they believe that it's more like to happen if they have put in time doing the mental visualization.

One study,[13] done at UCLA by Lien Pham and Shelly Taylor, explains the results of a psychological study that tells how mental stimulation or visualization help people go from point A to point B.

The researchers divided a class of students into three different groups who were all preparing for a upcoming midterm exam. The researchers asked the first group of students to simply imagine getting an A—*to focus on the ultimate outcome*—just seeing the final outcome and feel good about it. The second group of students were asked to do a complete mental visualization of each activity involved from that day until the date when the results come out. They needed to visualize *where and when they*

[13] https://icds.uoregon.edu/wp-content/uploads/2013/03/Harnessing-the-Imagination-Mental-Simulation-Self-regulation-and-Coping.pdf

would study, how they would handle the temptation to procrastinate, taking the exam itself, then the final test score, and rush of good feeling. A third group did neither of these and simply studied the way they were used to.

You see, while the first group was just focusing on the end goal, the second group needed to visualize or do a mental simulation of the entire process of looking at the obstacles, how to handle them, and finally getting a good score.

The results clearly spoke of the power of visualization. The first group of students scored about the same as the third group, but the second group, who mentally simulated the process of getting to a good grade for five minutes a day, scored eight points higher. The researchers therefore concluded that "visualizing success" decreases our motivation to actually do the work that leads to success. Students who ran mental simulations, on the other hand, showed better planning skills and less anxiety at test time.

Therefore, don't get trapped into the "outcome" visualization, rather focus on "process" visualization. Heidi Grant Halvorson, in her book *Succeed: How We Can Reach Our Goals,* explains in a similar way about visualization. She tells us:

"Don't visualize success. Instead, visualize the steps you will take in order to succeed. Just picturing yourself crossing the finish line doesn't actually help you get there— but visualizing how you run the race (the strategies you will use, the choices you will make, the obstacles you will face) not only will give you greater confidence, but also leave you better prepared for the task ahead. And that is definitely realistic optimism."

How should you do visualization?

Let's take an example of running a marathon to understand how you should carry out the process of visualization.

Before the race, visualize yourself running well—legs pumping like pistons, arms relaxed, breathing controlled. In your mind, break the course into sections and visualize how you will run each part, thinking about your pace, gait, and split time. Imagine what it will feel like when you hit "the wall," that point in the race where your body wants to stop, and more importantly, what you must do to break through it.

You may never run a marathon. However, you can use the same principles to achieve any goal—create a vivid mental picture of yourself succeeding in your actions, envision what you must do during each step of the process and, like a runner pushing through "the wall," use positive mental imagery to stay focused and motivated when you experience obstacles or setbacks.

Visualization cannot guarantee you success. It also does not replace hard work and practice. But when combined with diligent effort, it is a powerful way to achieve positive, behavioral change and create the life you desire.

The techniques suggested in this section go well beyond the realm of the known and explores the unknown and uncharted territories of your mind. You might have already heard that our conscious mind is just the "tip of the iceberg"—say, just 10% of our mind's abilities—while the remaining 90% is the subconscious mind. If you have ambitious goals of hacking your mind, then you need to discover and follow the approaches that go beyond the fathomable levels of your conscious mind. You need to explore and harness the potential of the mind at the deepest and subconscious levels of your mind.

Imagination and visualization give you an entirely new broad canvas and full liberty to create anything that you could imagine in your mind. Once you start exercising the power of imagination and then further do the simulations to achieve the goals you imagined, your subconscious mind will do all the heavy work of generating ideas, connecting the dots between different ideas, and present the options before you that you could have never found by merely paying attention at the conscious levels of your mind.

Now let's continue this journey and learn another technique in next chapter to get maximum benefits from the messages emerging from the deeper levels of our minds.

Chapter 8: Create Your Own Blueprint

****

"The pen is the tongue of the mind."

~ Horace

Get Your Ideas on Paper

We talked about geniuses like Einstein and Tesla to understand how imagination and visualization helped them tap into the infinite potential of their mind.

Now let's talk about one more legend, Thomas Edison, the inventor of the electric bulb and many other world-altering inventions. He received over 1,000 patents registered in his name. Though he was a prolific inventor, his biggest contribution appears to be the invention of the process of invention itself. Edison was a great believer of the power of the subconscious mind and how it can produce ideas quickly. And he used the ideas from his subconscious mind pretty well.

How, you ask?

He was known for his power nap strategy, as he used it wisely to tap the solutions from his subconscious mind. He would analyze complex problems, thinking rigorously over the ideas by consuming every piece of information on that problem, then he would strategically go into his power nap mode.

Our subconscious mind never sleeps; it's on duty every moment of your life. After all, it is responsible for ensuring that all bodily function of respiration, blood circulation, and digestion, etc. continues to happen during our sleep too. Napolean Hill once rightly mentioned, ""Your subconscious mind works continuously, while you are awake, and while you sleep."

Edison would drop the Pandora's box of questions onto his subconscious mind during that short power nap. He had put a bed in his office specifically for his power naps to take cues from his subconscious mind. Then, he would wake up from his nap, and guess what the first thing he used to do was. He would write the thoughts or ideas that were presented to him immediately on paper. After writing down those ideas, he'd reach out to his team of researchers to start conducting experiments on those ideas.

That's what he did his entire life—wrote as many ideas down as he could generate in his small notebook, which kept on forming the basis for his research and inventions. In fact, he exemplified the below quote:

Similarly, Richard Branson, the founder of Virgin Atlantics, is also known to keep a small diary with him all the time to keep track of different ideas popping into his head. Because he believed that ideas don't have a timetable, they don't come at a specific place or time; they are free birds. It's you who has to capture them when they present themselves, because once they are gone, it's difficult to invite them back.

This idea-capturing work needs to be very quick before they fly away. That's why they say, "Until it's on paper, it is vapor." You might have already heard that top corporate executives often brainstorm ideas during evening cocktails and chart out the plan on napkins. Only once you see it in front of you on paper, will you be able to plan out the finer details.

While imagination and simulation, which you learned about in the previous section, immerse you within yourself to mentally see the possibilities, the writing of your ideas is the first step toward bringing those ideas into fruition. In a way, writing is a bridge or gateway from mental thoughts to physical products. Every material world's manifestation has always had three stages. The first stage is the emerging of an idea in your head (through proper use of imagination and visualization) and the final stage is creation of the tangible product or service. But there is one important step in between, which is capturing that idea on paper and preparing a detailed blueprint of how it would look like and operate in reality.

Also, writing allows free space for your mind to generate more ideas. David Allen, the bestselling author of the book *Getting Things Done: The Art of Stress-Free Productivity*, emphasizes the importance of writing on paper and compares it to creating a "second mind outside" that you can refer to again, while keeping your mind free to focus on imagination and visualization.

Journaling

While we talked about writing down the thoughts or ideas that pop up in your mind, there is another way of making writing as a part of your daily habit. This habit is called journaling, where you write down your thoughts or ideas every day in a more systematic way.

There is enough literature out there that says our mind thinks approximately 60,000 thoughts daily. But the irony is that 95% of those thoughts are the same, which your mind keeps them repeating over and over again. This also means that, at any point in time, you would have only around 5 to 7 different thoughts. If you could capture these thoughts and write them down in your journal, then it will clear your head for better thinking and decision-making.

Also, journaling is considered amongst the most beneficial kind of writing. One 2005 study[14] found that the kind of "expressive

---

[14] http://apt.rcpsych.org/content/11/5/338.full

writing" often connected with journaling is especially therapeutic. The study found that participants who wrote about traumatic, stressful, or emotional events were significantly less likely to get sick, and were ultimately less seriously affected by trauma than their non-journaling counterparts.

Journaling activates the reticular activating system (RAS) in your brain, which is a bundle of nerves at our brainstem that filters out unnecessary information so the important stuff gets through. Our brains are consistently bombarded with millions of bytes of information every minute. It is not possible for our mind to let all the data and information in; hence it deploys a filtering system. RAS allows only that type of information that your mind finds most relevant.

For instance, you decide you would like to buy a new red Honda. Once you start thinking about the red Honda, from that day onward, you may notice more red Hondas on the street. It's not that suddenly people have started buying and driving more such cars, but it is your brain's RAS in play.

Therefore, once you put certain questions or thoughts in your mind and allow them to process in your head (remember, we talked about priming earlier), your mind starts taking notice about what is important for you and filters all other information as irrelevant and just presents before you the type of information that you've indicated as important.

Therefore, when you write specifically about your goals, dreams, and ambitions, you see it from your eyes in front of you on the paper, which in turn activates your RAS, and that makes you notice the relevant opportunities, which otherwise you will generally miss.

What should you write in your journal?

Hal Elrod, in his book *The Miracle Morning: The Not-So-Obvious Secret Guaranteed to Transform Your Life (Before 8AM)*, talks about six morning rituals that one should follow to kickstart the day with full energy and to optimize one's potential. He coins them in the form of an acronym S.A.V.E.R.S., which stands for Silence, Affirmation, Visualization, Exercise, Reading, and Scribble. The last one, scribbling, means journaling as a part of your morning routine.

He also specifically suggests what one should cover in one's journal, as follows:

- What are you grateful for regarding your previous day?
- What are your specific accomplishments?
- What are your specific areas of improvement?
- What are the top 5 things that you must do today to take your life to the next level?

If you want to know more about the ways of journaling, you will find this link https://www.robinsharma.com/article/how-to-keep-a-journal from Robin Sharma to get a detailed perspective of journal-writing and what it should contain.

Just to quickly recap: In the previous section, you learned about how to access the innate potential of your mind through imagination and visualization exercises. The current section was all about putting your ideas and thoughts in the material world. Even though you see those ideas on paper, it means they have the potential to become a physical reality.

Now is the time to put those ideas out in a real-world scenario. But here is the thing, when you get out in the world, you come across different kinds of people and different perspectives. While you may have only one perspective about the idea, there could be many other angles.

Therefore in the next step of your mind-hacking journey, we will specifically examine the different types of perspectives you need to keep in mind before you finally decide the best way to go forward with your idea.

Chapter 9: Master Multi-Perspective Thinking

****

> *"Sometimes all it takes is a tiny shift of perspective to see something familiar in a totally new light"*
>
> *~Dan Brown*

You often look at things from one specific perspective, and ignore all the other perspectives. Take a simple example. Assume you love to work out in the gym, but your spouse or partner hates going to gym, and he or she would rather walk or run outside. Assuming you get into debate of going to the gym versus exercising outside, you'd probably want to present plenty of reasons why going to the gym is a better option than running outside. You might argue:

- The gym has different types of equipment to train different parts of your body.

- You can strengthen different muscles by following specific exercise regimes.
- Rain, sun, or cold cannot prevent you from exercising at the gym.
- You can go to the gym at any time, but for going out you have to choose either early mornings or evenings only.
- You get to meet like-minded people with common health goals at the gym.
- You can get a trainer there to fine-tune your exercising needs, who can offer you tailor-made exercise routines most suitable for your body and goals.

You may continue on and on and on with the benefits. Like the way you have your own arguments, your partner or friend might have dozens of reasons to prefer going out and exercising in nature: running exposes you to nature, gives you access to fresh oxygen in the morning, the morning environment freshens your mood, running alone gives you an opportunity to connect with yourself better, etc.

Both of you might have good arguments to support your respective preferences, but here is the thing. If you continue to think only from one perspective, you'll never be able to understand your partner's perspective.

Above example was a pretty simple daily-life example, where two people can have a difference of outlook or perspective. But often life presents much more demanding situations, where it becomes utmost necessary to understand the other person's perspective. Take an example, if you don't like the way your boss expects you to perform or maybe you want your subordinate to perform in a particular situation. Here, you don't know what your boss or your subordinate is thinking in his mind, you don't understand their perspective, their personal circumstances, their way of working, the way they feel motivated to work, and so forth. The worst part is, without understanding the other person's perspective, we tend to make judgements about other people and start labelling them, which in turn makes it a never-resolving problem.

One of the key reasons for most of our problems is our inability to understand different perspectives. Each of us has a different way of looking at the world. It's like two different people standing outside on a sunny day, but wearing differently tinted sunglasses. Therefore, each will have a different version of how it looks outside, but there is only one reality.

In one of the previous sections on debugging your mind, we noted how the cognitive bias approach of our mind just keeps on searching for arguments to validate our own beliefs about something. We rarely try enough to understand the other perspective, which often leads to friction amongst partners, families, friends, work colleagues, etc. This difference of perspective and inability to look at things from another person's lenses not only delays the resolution of any particular problem, but also aggravates the problem by damaging our relationship with these people.

You can't think of harnessing the full potential of your mind if you don't develop the ability to think from different perspectives. Once you start thinking in different perspectives, you start to see the problem from many lenses; the natural progression of this understanding is—you don't argue with the person; rather you join hands to solve the problem holistically.

That's why Stephen R. Covey, in his legendary book *7 Habits of Highly Effective People*, has identified this as one of the most important habits, which is "seek first to understand, then to be understood."

How can you start developing multi-perspective thinking?

Sometimes the biggest problem is that we don't know what we don't know. If we don't really know that there could really be multiple ways of thinking about any problem, then first we need to address this as the root cause.

Edward de Bono, the author of *How to Have a Beautiful Mind* and a proponent of lateral thinking, devised a formula called "six thinking hats" to explain how you can develop multi-perspective thinking. The six thinking hats formula is to think about one problem from six different angles, so you don't miss any important aspects of the problem.

Let's understand with the example of a situation where four different people are standing in front of a building, but each on a different side of the building. Each one is given the task to describe the building's appearance, structure, and other details. After examining the building, the four people are required to meet each other and elaborate on the building, like the appearance, usage of glass, material, etc. Now please understand that all four people will have a different outlook on the building's appearance and therefore their descriptions will be unique to their overview of the building. Therefore, it is but obvious that each of them will have some difficulty in understanding the observations explained by the others.

Now, what's the best solution to understanding each other's perspective? The simplest solution is to make each person take one round of the building and have a look at the other three sides of the building. Once each person has looked at the other sides of the building, they can understand much better the different perspective on it.

The six thinking hats principle is similar to looking at a particular problem from six different angles before finalizing any solution of a given problem.

But why do we choose hats for this analogy? There is a reason behind this. A hat is something that you can easily take on and put off. If thinking is like a hat, then you know it's pretty flexible to wear any particular hat: you now own all six hats and use them as the need arises. You don't need to change your beliefs or assumptions to behave in a particular way. Therefore, the hat is a perfect metaphor for a flexible approach.

One more important point—given that the right side of our brain understands imagery better, it helps to remember these six hats by assigning colors to them. The colors of the six hats are white, red, black, yellow, green, and blue. Each hat represents a different perspective of looking at things. Let's understand how each of these hats works specifically.

1. The White Hat

The white color will remind you of white paper—a blank canvas—which means there needs to be something written first on this paper. The white thinking hat requires you to compile more information because only after you have some information, can you think about analyzing it. This hat requires you to ascertain the facts. If the question in your mind is what business idea you should pick up to start your venture, or whether you should take up a particular job or not, this white hat is the most necessary hat to start with.

You are required to acquire lot of information at this stage, like what is the size of the industry, how are the market trends, who are the main competitors, what are your current skills sets, and what do you need to learn more to get this business started, how much investment is needed, what's the margin, would you go solo or engage a partner for this venture, etc.

Whenever you come across any problem or situation, you need to put on the white hat first, which will prompt you to seek out as much information as you can about the problem. This is all factual information, meaning if you reached the office at 9:05 a.m., the factual information is you're five minutes late to the office. This hat doesn't get into the reasons, suggestions, feelings, etc. (for those, we have a different hat coming up later). Analyze the information and determine the gaps you have and what you can deduce from the information you currently have. It's fact that a lack of basic information is the primary cause of not being able to make correct decisions.

Collect as much information as possible given the time available to you, but don't be at the other extreme, where you just keep on collecting information and don't make any decision. Beware of this. The idea here is not to make haphazard decisions based on half-baked information and use some precaution, but to be aware not to be over-cautious where you just keep collecting information to make a "perfect" decision. Remember the 40-70 rule in a previous chapter.

2. The Red Hat

The red color symbolizes warmth and hotness and this red thinking-hat requires you to consider your feelings about the problem in front of you. This hat is your emotional hat. This hat requires you to be intuitive or instinctive and listen to your gut reactions or statements of emotional feeling, without thinking about any rationale or justification.

After putting on this hat, you ask yourself, "how do I feel about it? What does my gut say about going ahead with a particular person in business partnership? Why doesn't it feel right to hire this particular person?" Most of the time, such feelings don't have any reason; they simply come out of your intuition. When you put the red hat on, there is no room for reasoning—only plain feelings coming from your heart and gut (we will use a different hat to take reasoning and logic into account).

In any serious decision, people don't often use their feelings or emotions for moving ahead, rather they want to seem more logical and rational in their decisions. But there are certain situations where you don't have any other option except to trust your gut or intuition and make decisions. In fact, when there is lack of information due to venturing into the unchartered territories, most high-achievers treat their intuition as a treasured asset and take decisions based on what feels right to them. If you are a "head" person and not a "heart" person, you may tend to ignore this perspective— but paying attention to the emotional aspects of the things has the potential to reveal certain other aspects, which you'd find very difficult to understand with your rational mind. Therefore, trust in the process and take into account this aspect— try to listen to what *feels* right or wrong to you.

3. The Black Hat

The next one is the black hat, which is the most commonly used hat in our day-to-day interactions and behavior. This hat represents critical thinking; you use your logic and judgment to find out what could be wrong in any situation. The purpose of this hat is to safeguard you from things that might go wrong when you make a particular decision. The black hat represents caution and prompts questioning whether the alternatives available in front of you match the parameters you have chosen for a particular decision.

Suppose you are thinking of quitting your current job to take up another job. This hat requires you to look at things in the new job that might not fit with your personal values. You might assess certain things in your prospective job that you wouldn't like, despite the job offering you a much higher salary package.

While the white hat required you to collect more facts and information about the topic at hand, the black hat requires you to critically assess the situation. It requires you to ask things that might go wrong to help you choose the right alternative. But you shouldn't be using this hat solely with the objective of finding fault as an excuse to reject the idea. The objective here is to be objective, while critically examining the situation and basing your decision on the facts about the problem.

4. The Yellow Hat

Frankly speaking, this hat is not frequently used in our day-to-day lives. We live in a modern world where everybody is just trying to prove their argument as right and make other realize that they are wrong. It's like a court room situation, where the litigator's only job is to find fault with the other side's arguments and even intentionally hide his own negative points to win the litigation. Okay, but that's the necessity of legal battles. This does more harm than good if we apply this formula while using our thinking abilities.

The yellow hat's role is exactly the opposite of the black hat. This hat requires you to look at the brighter side; here, you look for value, benefits, and all the positive points in a given situation.

Take an example. If you hear about some regular guy who drops out of college without being sure of his future, just to test out his gut-felt ground-breaking business idea, your instant reaction will be to ridicule him. You will advise him with the "first things first" rule: You will tell him to complete his education first, and then think about pursuing something else so that he has a safety net in case things don't go according to plan, he can get a job with that education. Now, if you observe carefully, you just wore the black hat. But the yellow hat will demand of you to find the benefits and values out of this situation. Probably, your mind will remind you of many college dropouts, who never thought of formal education as the only roadmap, and rather built massive businesses to even offer jobs to college graduates.

The yellow hat thinking invites you to find advantages in the situation at hand. Don't ignore this hat, rather use it in all situations by gathering information about what is already good in the situation, and how you can benefit more out of that situation. For some people, getting laid off from their job paves the way to the entrepreneurial world and offers them the financial and time freedom, which they wouldn't have ever thought otherwise. Every situation has two sides, so it's recommended to use this yellow hat to look at the opportunities and advantages out of any situation.

5. The Green Hat

Think of green as nature, vegetation, and thus growth. The green thinking hat demands you to be creative and offer ideas and suggestions for solving any problem. You need to come up with possibilities and alternatives to ponder upon different ways of doing the things.

This is the possibility thinking hat. This hat requires you to dream and think about ways to make things happen. Whether your ideas are practical or not is not the problem with this hat; you just need to release your creative juices. The job of this hat is to open up your mind to the possibilities around. This requires imagination. Remember the message from Einstein from the previous section, when he said, "Imagination is better than knowledge."

While the white hat requires you to collect factual information about the problem at hand—for example, how far is the manufacturing plant from the distributors of any particular product—it will ask you factual data about tell how many miles away, the green hat will demand of you to come up with ideas. You'd ask yourself, is there any other route where you can shorten the travel distance, or could you use drones to deliver your products to the distributors, or is it possible to use some means of transport where, due to cheaper fuel, you can reduce the distribution cost? This hat is all about scratching your head to activate imagination and come up with fresh new ideas to look at the problem. This

option increases the possibilities or
alternatives, which then would need to be
looked at by again putting on the white,
black, red, or yellow hat.

6. The Blue Hat

Now comes the last one—the blue thinking
hat.

De Bono compares the blue thinking hat
with "blue sky," which means a top-level
view at 40,000 feet up, or an overview of
the broader picture. By now, you'd have
realized that most people generally put only
a few types of hats on. Some just wear a
black hat—always looking at the negative
and thus not taking any action. Others
might just use the yellow hat and run the
risk of being trapped into positive thinking,
being ignorant of real risks involved in the
situations.

The blue thinking hat plays the role of
organizing various hats in your thinking
process. In any decision-making process,
the blue hat plays the role of setting the
focus. The blue hat prompts you to focus on
the immediate question at hand. It
determines the focal point of the discussion

and asks you, "What is the problem? What do we want to think about and decide?"

Once you start, the blue hat controls the organization of various thinking hats. The blue hat sets the sequence of putting specific hats on, one after the other and keeps generating the points out of each discussion. When sitting among a group of people discussing the problem, the blue hat organizes the discussion and reminds people, "No, we are talking with the yellow hat on now, and the point you have made is with the red hat." Or "Please come up with some more green hat ideas, as we need to figure out the best alternatives."

The blue hat is more of a controlling hat. It's like the conductor of orchestra, to get a melodious music playing out of different instruments at one time. The better you organize the sequence of these hats, the better you develop your multi-perspective understanding of the problem. The results are the holistically improved decision-making.

To sum up, the thinking hats metaphor offers a more complete and elaborate segregation of the various thinking directions you should go to strengthen your decision-making muscle. The more you start using different thinking perspectives in your life, the more you will develop your cognitive abilities, improve relationships, and come up with holistic solutions to complex problems.

With that, we will now move on to the last section of this book, which requires you to look outside of your mind. Yes, now we will look at different aspects of your body, which, if nurtured well, will sharpen your brain's abilities.

Chapter 10: Your Body – The Key to Genius Mind

****

"Take care of your body. It's the only place you have to live."

— Jim Rohn

Who hasn't heard the wonderful saying below while growing up?

"A healthy mind stays in a healthy body."

This is absolutely correct, because without all your body's organs working perfectly, your mind won't be able to perform at its optimum level. Your mind needs energy, oxygen supply, and vibrant blood flow to the brain to perform at the best level.

However, we often ignore the importance of physical health and think that our work comes first. We neglect our physical health only to see later that it has ultimately deteriorated our mental performance. How often have you been sold to your own excuses like the ones below?

- I don't have time to exercise even for 15 minutes a day.
- Oh, I can't afford sleeping more than four hours. There is so much to do and so little time.
- I need to have a working lunch today—a large pizza and few hamburgers would be good. And yeah, they will help for evening snacks too, if my work takes that long.

Precisely, a lot of people think that spending any time thinking or making any efforts to nurture our bodies is additional work, and we see this as hurdle or hindrance to our productivity and achieving more.

But in reality, this is like someone saying, "I need to drive the car faster to reach my destination sooner. I really don't have time to stop at the gas station to get the fuel." And you know what will happen. Eventually, the fuel tank will be empty and or her key objective will be to find fuel to move this car. But we do the same thing with our body. We are in such a hurry to run the race of achieving our goals that we generally forget that our body is our sole vehicle to reach there.

We understand this at an intellectual level only, but do not implement this advice in our life sincerely. If you still reading, it clearly means you are sincere about hacking the full potential of your mind. Therefore, engrain this principle into your mind that only if you take care of your body, you'll be able to exploit the full power of your mind.

I don't want to overwhelm you with too much, but there are three most important areas of your body that you must take care of, which are:

1. Diet
2. Exercise
3. Sleep

In all the previous sections of the book, you learned about the various strategies to build you mental muscles, which can do the heavy-lifting to make your mind sharper. But I know you are here for holistic results, not some piecemeal short spurt of productivity. Life is not a sprint, it's a marathon—and you want long-term sustainable results.

The above three factors are the three pillars for your vibrant health, like a tripod on which you are putting your high quality DSLR camera. If you don't have a tripod under your camera or if one of the legs of your tripod is broken, you won't be able to take high-quality images. You picture might be blurry or slanted, if any of the legs is unbalanced. Similarly, if you ignore any of the three important aspects of your body, then it'll have adverse impact on your mind. You won't be able to utilize the full potential of your mind.

Let's now understand each pillar of your health and how you should take care of them.

1. Diet

"You are what you eat."

I was watching some video from Jaggi Vasudev, an Indian yogi, mystic, and bestselling author, also famously known as Sadhguru. He asked the question to someone, "Do you know how to convert a banana into a human being? Then he said everyone has the potential to turn a banana into a human being. This intrigued me instantly about what he was going to say further. "When you eat banana, it doesn't remain banana any more, it becomes a part of you," he said. The particles of the banana now convert into your flesh, blood, and energy, and now the banana is a part of the human being, meaning that the banana is now a human being.

What an amazing and different perspective, isn't it? But this brings forth one more interesting point. It means whatever traits any particular food has; you assume those traits within you just by eating that food. The way different human beings have different nature, every food item also has its own nature and benefits.

If you are eating burgers, pizzas, and other fast food items, they will have a different impact on your body as compared to eating green vegetables and fresh salads. You might have already experienced and seen the difference.

Of course, a healthy mind stays in a healthy body. But the foundation to a healthy body is healthy food. Food is the primary source of our energy. While exercise and sleep stimulate and rejuvenate our body, it is food that gives the nutrition and energy to our body in the first place. While different foods are necessary for optimum health of different parts of our body, there are some specific foods that generate special benefits for our mind.

Here is a list of healthy foods for the brain, suggested by webMD.com in one article[15] entitled "Eat Smart For A Healthier Brain." Below is a list of few most important foods, which will directly cater your need for a healthy brain and the benefits thereof:

- **Blueberries.** In many animal studies, researchers have found that blueberries help protect the brain from oxidative stress and may reduce the effects of age-related conditions such as Alzheimer's disease or dementia. Studies have also shown that diets rich in blueberries significantly improved both the learning capacity and motor skills of aging rats, making them

[15] https://www.webmd.com/diet/features/eat-smart-healthier-brain#1

mentally equivalent to much younger rats.

That's why they call it "brainberries" too. Ann Kulze, MD, author of *Dr. Ann's 10-Step Diet: A Simple Plan for Permanent Weight Loss & Lifelong Vitality*, recommends adding at least 1 cup of blueberries a day in any form— fresh, frozen, or freeze-dried.

- **Nuts and seeds.** Nuts and seeds are good sources of vitamin E. Higher levels of vitamin E correspond to less cognitive decline as you get older. Add an ounce a day of walnuts, hazelnuts, Brazil nuts, filberts, almonds, cashews, peanuts, sunflower seeds, sesame seeds, flax seed, or unhydrogenated nut butters such as peanut butter, almond butter, and tahini—it could be raw or roasted.

- **Avocados.** Avocados are almost as good as blueberries in promoting brain health. Though avocado is a fatty fruit, it's a monounsaturated fat, which contributes to healthy blood flow, which means a healthy brain.

Avocados also lower blood pressure and, as hypertension is a risk factor for the decline in cognitive abilities, a lower blood pressure should promote brain health. Avocados are high in calories, however, so it is advised by experts to add just 1/4 to 1/2 of an avocado to one daily meal as a side dish.

- **Whole grains.** Whole grains, such as oatmeal, whole-grain breads, and brown rice can reduce the risk for heart disease. Every organ in the body is dependent on blood flow. If you promote cardiovascular health, you're promoting good flow to the organ system, which includes the brain. While wheat germ is not technically a whole grain, it is still a recommended food, because in addition to fiber, it has vitamin E and some omega-3s. Experts suggest 1/2 cup of whole-grain cereal, 1 slice of bread two to three times a day, or 2 tablespoons of wheat germ a day.

- **Beans.** Beans stabilize glucose (blood sugar) levels. The brain is dependent on glucose for fuel and since it can't store the glucose, it relies on a steady stream of energy, which beans can provide. Any bean will do and it is recommended to consume 1/2 cup every day.

- **Pomegranate juice.** Pomegranate juice (or you can eat the fruit itself) offers potent antioxidant benefits, which protect the brain from the damage of free radicals. "Probably no part of the body is more sensitive to the damage from free radicals as the brain," says board-certified neurologist David Perlmutter, MD, author of *The Better Brain Book*.

  Citrus fruits and colorful vegetables are also high on Perlmutter's list of "brainy" foods because of their antioxidant properties—"the more colorful the better," he says. Experts recommend approximately 2 ounces a day, diluted with spring water or seltzer.

- **Freshly brewed tea.** Two to three cups a day of freshly brewed tea—hot or iced —contains a modest amount of caffeine and can boost brain power by enhancing memory, focus, and mood. Tea also has potent antioxidants, especially the class known as catechines, which promotes healthy blood flow. Bottled or powdered teas don't work, it has to be freshly brewed—and tea bags can also work.

- **Wild salmon.** Deep-water fish, such as salmon, are rich in omega-3 essential fatty acids, which are essential for brain function. Omega-3s also contain anti-inflammatory substances. It is recommended to have a 4-ounce serving, two to three times a week.

- **Dark chocolate.** Dark chocolate has powerful antioxidant properties, contains several natural stimulants, including caffeine, which enhance focus and concentration, and stimulates the production of endorphins, which helps improve mood. One-half ounce to 1 ounce a day will provide all the benefits you need.

If you nurture your body with the food directly benefitting your brain, you are already ahead in your game by creating a solid infrastructure for your mind, which will definitely boost your brain's ability to the next level.

2. Exercise

Our bodies are not designed to be stationary else God would have made us trees. We are given legs, so there is some purpose. In fact, everything created by God has some purpose, though we may not understand fully, but there is a bigger universal plan, of which we are just a part of.

In fact, in the primitive ages, it was our moving ability that enabled us to hunt for food. It also helped us to run away from dangerous animals and protect ourselves in dense dangerous forests. The Industrial Age created a huge demand for manual labour, and again our ability to move and work with our hands provided the food on our table. Then came the information age, where our brain became the chief operating officer of our bodies and the requirement of moving our body is now heavily reduced. Today, you can sit for hours and still you have the ability to earn the money. But this approach has taken a toll on our physical and mental health. The cases of obesity, stress, and depression are higher than ever.

But, in your quest to hack your mind and tap its full potential, you can't ignore the benefits of exercise. Exercise is not only necessary to keep your entire body healthy by allowing the proper digestion of food, thus generating the adequate energy, it is much more important when it comes to nourishing our brains.

John Ratey in his book *Spark: The Revolutionary New Science of Exercise and Brain* states that exercise is truly our best defence against everything from depression to ADD to addiction to menopause to Alzheimer's. The book explores comprehensively the connection between exercise and the brain. He states in the book:

> Physical activity sparks biological changes that encourage brain cells to bind to one another. For the brain to learn, these connections must be made; they reflect the brain's fundamental ability to adapt to challenges. The more neuroscientists

discover about this process, the clearer it becomes that exercise provides an unparalleled stimulus, creating an environment in which the brain is ready, willing, and able to learn.

A regular exercise regime stimulates the release of positive neurotransmitters, like dopamine (which encourages motivation, attention, and pleasure), serotonin (which enhances learning, mood, and self-esteem), and norepinephrine (which leads to arousal and alertness). The best part- exercise expedites the production of BDNF (brain-derived neurotrophic factor), a protein which Ratey has dubbed "Miracle-Gro for the brain"

In fact, researchers found that if they sprinkled BDNF onto neurons in a petri dish, the cells automatically sprouted new branches, producing the same structural growth required for learning.

Also, Kelly McGonigal, a psychologist and researcher explains, "When neuroscientists have peered inside the brains of new exercisers, they have seen increase in both gray matter—brain cells—and white matter, the insulation on brain cells that help them communicate quickly and efficiently with each other. Physical exercise—like meditation—makes your brain bigger and faster, and the prefrontal cortex shows the largest training effect."

Scientists have also discovered lately an "exercise hormone" called Irisin, which is linked to improved health and cognitive function. Researchers found that the part of the brain that responds strongly to aerobic exercise is the hippocampus. There have been experiments conducted, which show that the structure of hippocampus increases when you get fitter physically. Since the hippocampus is at the core of the brain's learning and memory systems, it has memory-boosting effects due to improved cardiovascular fitness.[16]

---

[16] https://www.psychologytoday.com/blog/the-athletes-way/201404/physical-activity-improves-cognitive-function

The above research is enough to convince you that exercising is one of greatest tool to hack the limitless potential of your brain.

There is no specific exercise that I can recommend you, because everyone is different and has different exercise needs. But I liked the approach Tony Robbins, one of the most sought-out strategy coach, suggests, which saves times as well as gives you intensive exercise as well in just 15 minutes. Just have a look at this Youtube video named <u>Tony Robbins' workout routine is 15 minutes of pure torture</u>[17].

3. Sleep:

Now let's talk about the last but the most important pillar of your physical existence. Sleep is not just lying down idle in bed for 8 hours, as some people might think. You might have heard some people advocating that you spend one-third of your life sleeping and doing nothing, as if suggesting that sleep is a waste of time.

But this is all a fallacy. There is enough research now to establish that if you <u>consistently compromise</u> and deprive

[17] https://www.youtube.com/watch?v=pzBGScXEs9k

yourself from the required number of sleep hours every night, you are already in the grip of stress and anxiety.

Sleep deprivation studies repeatedly show a variable (negative) impact on mood, cognitive performance, and motor function due to an increasing sleep propensity and destabilization of the wake state. Specific neurocognitive domains, including executive attention, working memory, and divergent higher cognitive functions are particularly vulnerable to sleep loss.

Lack of sleep zaps willpower because if you are sleep-deprived then your cells have trouble absorbing glucose from the main bloodstream. This lack of glucose makes them under-fueled and exhausted. In such exhausting situations, our brain wants to conserve the energy for the body's normal operations, as there is low stock of energy, and it therefore it wants to retain enough for any emergency situation.

Moreover, our prefrontal cortex, responsible for executive functions like focus, memory, and making decisions, suffers the most due to this lack of energy caused by sleep deprivation. The studies[18] also suggest that sleep loss produces temporary changes in cerebral metabolism, cognition, emotion, and behavior that is something equivalent to mild prefrontal dysfunction.

Isn't this scary enough?

Look at the history and how the legends used sleep to their advantage. As you read already, Edison was famous for taking power naps during the day. Winston Churchill was famous for creating "two fresh mornings" every day with the small naps called power naps during the day, during the entire WWII, where he led his country from the brink of defeat to victory.

There is a reason why ultra-performers give so much weight to sleep. Sleep gives the required rest to your body and brain to recover. It repairs the damaged cells and rejuvenates the body. In fact, sleep is an important element to grow your body and mind. Jim Loehr, the famous performance psychologist in his book *Toughness Training for Life* gives the formula for growth. He states:

[18] https://www.ncbi.nlm.nih.gov/pubmed/17765011

It's important to understand that only rarely does the volume of stress defeat us; **far more often the agent of defeat is insufficient capacity for recovery after the stress**. Great stress simply requires great recovery. Your goal in toughness, therefore, is to be able to spike powerful waves of stress followed by equally powerful troughs of recovery. So here is an essential Toughness Training Principle: Work hard. Recover equally hard.

His formula is Stress + Recovery = Growth. He puts it this way:

"Precisely stress is the stimulus for growth. **Recovery is when you grow**."

This is really an amazing principle for mind hackers; you need to exercise to your mind, but then let it rest in order for you to grow.

In your endeavour to exploit the fullest potential of your mind, focus on ensuring you get the right quantity and quality of sleep every night. How much should I sleep, and how can I ensure quality sleep, you ask?

Notably, National Sleep Foundation in its study[19] about sleep time duration and recommendations came out with the results below about the minimum number of hours of sleep required for people of different age groups. The study panel agreed that, for healthy individuals with normal sleep, the appropriate sleep duration should be as follows:

    a. For newborns, between 14 and 17 hours
    b. Infants, between 12 and 15 hours
    c. Toddlers, between 11 and 14 hours
    d. Preschoolers, between 10 and 13 hours
    e. School-aged children, between 9 and 11 hours
    f. Teenagers, between 8 to 10 hours
    g. 7 to 9 hours for young adults and adults

[19] https://www.sleephealthjournal.org/article/S2352-72181500015-7/fulltext

h. 7 to 8 hours of sleep for older adults

How to get quality sleep

Deepak Chopra, the author of bestselling book *The Seven Spiritual Laws of Success*, suggests some great tips for getting a restful night's sleep as below:

- Eat only a light meal in the evening, before 7:30, if possible.

- Go for a leisurely walk after dinner

- Be in bed by 10 p.m.

- Download your thoughts from the day in a journal before going to bed so that your mind doesn't keep you awake.

Also, in his book *Sleep Smarter*, Shawn Stevenson explained that the timing between 10 pm into 12 midnight is the best to get in your bed. After that time, you find it very difficult to get into sleep mode.

Also, the room you sleep in should be dark. It's best for you if you could avoid keeping your phone in your room. If not, then at least keep it away at such distance that you have to get out of your bed to check it. And remember, all notifications should be on silent mode, except the phone ring, which you may keep on for emergency matters.

So the formula to a healthy body and eventually to a robust mind is to eat well, exercise regularly, and have enough sleep, and this will provide the strong foundation and infrastructure to create a robust mind. With vibrant body built on three strong pillars and fully equipped with effective mental strategies, no one can stop you from harnessing the fullest potential of your mind.

Conclusion

"Old ways won't open the new doors."
~ Anonymous

Congratulations, you made it to the end. People who finish what they start deserve applause. I literally stopped writing and just applauded for you. You also should reward yourself with your own pat on your back, because you disciplined yourself and put sincere efforts to work toward learning something important to transform your life.

I sincerely hope you find yourself now equipped with effective strategies to start unleashing your mind's untapped capabilities. You might have already realized some principles stated in the book are such that merely knowing about them has the impact of broadening your thinking horizon. That's good, but it's not enough. You and I who are in this personal development journey obviously know that it requires enough practice of the principles to attain the stages of self mastery.

None of us started running immediately after coming out of mother's womb; it involved a whole arduous process of learning, crawling, falling, getting up and again trying before you started walking. Similarly there is no short-cut or some pill available out there that you swallow and next day, you become a different person. It's an evolutionary process. And the process requires some work. Awareness of the right principles are definitely the right place to start, but mere awareness will not do. It's the sincere practice and implementation that will take you to far places.

I genuinely believe you must have got enough wisdom nuggets from this book. The secrets of geniuses and high-achievers are not hidden from you now. It only requires you implement those principles in your life to see the impressive changes and results in your life. The hidden and untapped potentials of your mind are just waiting for you on the other side of your actions.

My only wish for you is to take utmost advantage of this precious tool called the "mind" and start transforming your life.

I wish you all the best.

Som

Your Free Gift:

Did you download your Free Gift already?

Click Below and Download your **Free Report**

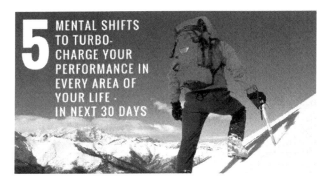

Learn 5 Mental Shifts To Turbo-Charge Your Performance In Every Area Of Your Life - in Next 30 Days!

You can also grab your FREE GIFT Report through this below URL:

http://sombathla.com/mentalshifts

Copyright © 2018 by Som Bathla

DISCLAIMER

While all attempts have been made to verify the information provided in this publication, the author does not assume any responsibility for errors, omissions, or contrary interpretations of the subject matter herein.

The views expressed are those of the author alone, and should not be taken as expert instruction or commands. The reader is responsible for his or her own actions.

The author makes no representations or warranties with respect to the accuracy or completeness of the contents of this work and specifically disclaims all warranties, including without limitation warranties of fitness for a particular purpose. No warranty may be created or extended by sales or promotional materials. The advice and recipes contained herein may not be suitable for everyone. This work is sold with the understanding that the author is not engaged in rendering medical, legal or other professional advice or services. If professional assistance is required, the services of a competent professional person should be sought. The author shall not be liable for damages arising here from. The fact that an individual, organization of website is referred to in this work as a citation and/or potential source of further information does not

174

mean that the author endorses the information the individual, organization to website may provide or recommendations they/it may make. Further, readers should be aware that Internet websites listed in this work might have changed or disappeared between when this work was written and when it is read.

Adherence to all applicable laws and regulations, including international, federal, state, and local governing professional licensing, business practices, advertising, and all other aspects of doing business in any jurisdiction in the world is the sole responsibility of the purchaser or reader.

28458724R00103

Printed in Poland
by Amazon Fulfillment
Poland Sp. z o.o., Wrocław